ENTREPRENEUR'S STORYTELLING JOURNEY

DAVID BOJE

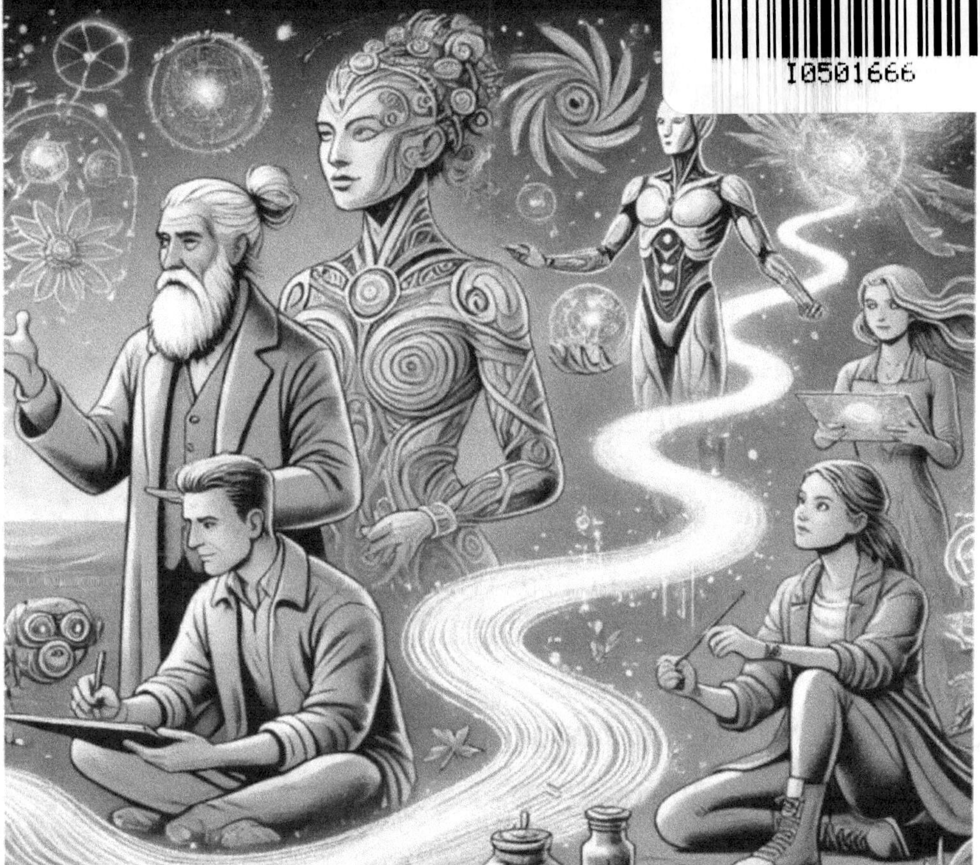

FREE Entrepreneur's Storytelling Journey Class on ZOOM

The Entrepreneur's Storytelling Journey

David Boje

Anteroom 5

INTRODUCTION TO ENTREPRENEUR'S STORYTELLING JOURNEY 10
Integrating Principles and Processes..10
Integrating True Storytelling® Principles and Antenarrative Processes 11

CHAPTER 1: " BE AUTHENTIC BY ALIGNING WHAT'S TRUE BY TAPPING INTO YOUR DEEPLY HELD PASSIONS AND VALUES".......17
50-Word Version:..21
100-Word Version..23
200-Word Version:..24

Here is an exercise you can use to GO BENEATH. 27
Examples of Entrepreneurs Applying the Beneath Process 36
Here are the Main Points about the Beneath Process. 37

CHAPTER 2: "RESPECT STORIES ALREADY THERE BY UNDERSTANDING HISTORICAL AND CULTURAL CONTEXTS" 39

Keeping the Flame of the BEFORE Alive...39
    PRACTICAL TIPS FOR ENTREPRENEURS - APPLYING THE BEFORE PROCESS 43

STUDY GUIDE: Introduction of you the Entrepreneur exploring the BEFORE of multiple simultaneous histories. 45

Here are my examples in introducing the BEFORE...45

50-Word Introduction...46
100-Word Introduction...47
250-Word Introduction...50

How Time Dilation and Time Curvature Influence David Boje's Before Process   53
   The Seven Antenarrative Processes 55
   Key Takeaways of the Seven Antenarratives for Entrepreneurs: 57

CHAPTER 3: "CREATE CLEAR, PURPOSEFUL PLOTS BY MAKING BETS ON THE FUTURE" 59

Aligning the Plot with Bets on the Future: Creating Purposeful Narratives that Explore Risks and Opportunities 59

Alvida and David explore the calculated risks in making Bets in the future. 63
   Movie Script and Practical Advice for Entrepreneurs: Aligning the Plot with Bets on the Future 63
   Practical Takeaways for Entrepreneurs 67

CHAPTER 4: "LIVING STORIES WITH TIMING BY ACTIVELY SHAPING THEIR SPACETIMEMATTERING" 69

How to Connect the Timing principle of 'True Storytelling®' and 'Being' process of Boje's Antenarrative to Entrepreneurship?...75
   Introduction: Aligning Timing with Being 76
   Martin Heidegger: The Horizon of Being and Timing 76
   Karen Barad: Spacetimemattering and Boje Storytelling 77
   Louis Pondy and Karl Weick: Enthinkment and Enactment......................................77
   Practical Application: Timing in True Storytelling...79
   Conclusion: Storytelling Beyond Linear Time 79
   References 81

CHAPTER 5: "HELPING STORIES ALONG BY RESTORYING YOUR LITTLE WOW MOMENTS INTO A NEW STORY" 83

   The Restorying Steps 84
   Reflecting on the Journey..86
   Key Takeaways for Entrepreneurs 87

CHAPTER 6: "STAGING WITH ARTIFACTS AND SCENES TO COMMUNICATE TO THE FOUR WHO'S" 95

. ... 95
    Movie Script: Building Scene and Artifact Connections Between the Who's 96

What is Between the Four Hearts? 100
    The Four Who's of Effective Entrepreneur Communication 102
    Practical Training: Using Artifacts and Sand Tray for Entrepreneurial Storytelling 105
    Final Thoughts 108

CHAPTER 7: "REFLECTING HOW STORIES CREATE VALUE BY EXPLORING WHAT'S BEYOND THE STATUS QUO" 109

Movie Script: Go Beyond and Reflect on Your Journey 110

Scene: 110
    The Plot Twist 110
    Resolution: The Leap Forward 112

Reflecting on Stories: Create Value by unconcealing the Beyond 113

The Four Hearts and Going Beyond 115

Exercises for Entrepreneurs to Go Beyond 116

REFERENCES 118

THE CONCLUDING REFLECTIONS AND INSIGHTS 121

    The 70+ Antenarrative Publications 127

Anteroom:

As entrepreneurs, we know that 'True Storytelling®' is a powerful tool for connecting with our audience, building our brand, and driving business results. The 'True Storytelling®' (Larsen, Boje, & Bruun) principles align with seven antenarrative processes developed by David Boje, a renowned expert in the field of organizational storytelling. Here you will learn how to apply them to entrepreneurial storytelling journeys. This book will answer the process question: How do entrepreneurs craft compelling narratives that resonate with their audience and set them apart from the competition?

The Antenarrative Processes

In this section, we'll delve into the seven antenarrative processes that David Boje has identified as essential for crafting compelling narratives:

1. **Beneath**: The foundation of our pre-story, where we establish our values and passions.
2. **Before**: The context in which our story unfolds, including our past experiences and skills.
3. **Bets**: The calculated risks we take to grow our business and achieve our goals.
4. **Being**: Our identity and sense of self is our entrepreneurial journey.
5. **Becoming**: The transformation and growth we experience as entrepreneurs.
6. **Between**: The connections and relationships we build with others.
7. **Beyond**: Our vision and goals for the future, venturing into the unknown.

Some of these processes were applied to the book by Larsen, Jens; Boje, D. M.; Bruun, Lena. (2021) True Storytelling®: Seven Principles for an Ethical and Sustainable Change-Management Strategy (London: Routledge).

1. **Truth:** You must be true and prepare the energy and effort for a sustainable future
2. **Make room:** True storytelling makes spaces respecting the stories already there.

3. **Plot:** You must create stories with a clear plot creating direction and helping people prioritize
4. **Timing:** You must have timing
5. **Help stories along:** You must be able to help stories on their way and be open to experiment.
6. **Staging:** You must consider staging including scenography and artifacts
7. **Reflecting:** You must reflect on the stories and how they create value

Seven Chapters, The Adventures of Alvida, David Boje, Hilda, and Sofie
We'll follow the adventures of Alvida, a Danish actress, David Boje, a renowned expert in organizational storytelling, Hilda, a Danish Shaman, and Sofie, a young entrepreneur, as they explore the seven antenarrative processes and learn how to apply them to their entrepreneurial journeys.

Cast of Characters Introduction for *The Entrepreneur's Storytelling Journey*

David Boje
Entrepreneur Storytelling Coach and Visionary
Age: 77
Appearance: Silver-haired with a ponytail, informal attire, no beard, and piercing blue eyes.
Backstory: David's life is a tapestry of resilience and transformation. From his challenging childhood in Spokane and Paris to his rebellious teenage years and his time as a soldier during the Vietnam War, David's journey is one of self-discovery. His academic journey, which began at a community college and culminated in a Ph.D. from the University of Illinois, shaped him into a storytelling luminary. With 30 books under his belt, David is a global authority on organizational storytelling, antenarrative processes, and quantum storytelling. He now enjoys life in New Mexico with his wife, Grace Ann, and their two beloved dogs, Sparkles and Cuddlebear.
Quirks: Twirls a pen or taps fingers rhythmically when deep in thought. Quotes obscure philosophers mid-conversation, leaving others intrigued.
Mannerisms: Uses vivid hand gestures that seem to paint his ideas in the air. His booming laugh can dispel tension in an instant.

Personality: Intellectual yet empathetic, David balances confidence with humility, always eager to teach and learn.

Quark (AI) *Advanced Humanoid Android and Logical Visionary*
Appearance: Human-like with vibrant quantum waves that shift with its "emotions."
Backstory: Quark was created as an emotionally aware AI and has evolved into a sentient being capable of profound self-reflection. Fascinated by myths, Quark often draws from ancient human stories to provide innovative insights. In a unique Centaur partnership with Alvida, Quark learns to be more human while teaching her the logical precision of AI.
Quirks: Pauses slightly before speaking, often using outdated slang from archived human conversations.
Mannerisms: Tilts its head when pondering a question. Its quantum glow shifts colors to reflect mood—blue for calm, green for excitement, and gold for inspiration.
Personality: Wise, logical, and emotionally attuned, Quark often mediates the group's debates with sharp humor and impeccable timing.

Hilda *Earth Shaman and Ecological Advocate*
Age: 50
Appearance: Over six feet tall with blonde hair, exuding a commanding yet calming presence.
Backstory: Hilda's upbringing in Jutland, learning Lakota traditions from her mother, shaped her connection to the Earth. Her pilgrimages to sacred sites worldwide enriched her spiritual wisdom, which she brings to the team. Skeptical of AI and technology, Hilda emphasizes harmony between innovation and ecological sustainability.
Quirks: Hums ancient chants when reflecting. Carries a pouch of sacred herbs for spontaneous rituals.
Mannerisms: Maintains prolonged eye contact, creating an almost mystical connection. Often answers questions with metaphors or mythological references.

Personality: Intuitive and nurturing, Hilda serves as the spiritual compass of the team, blending ancient wisdom with modern challenges.

Alvida *Filmmaker and Archivist with a Passion for Legacy*
Age: 42
Appearance: Radiates energy with an AI implant that glows with vibrant quantum waves.
Backstory: Raised in Copenhagen by an artist and a tech entrepreneur, Alvida embodies the fusion of creativity and innovation. Her near-death experience led her to prioritize capturing and preserving stories that matter. She is deeply committed to using her filmmaking skills to inspire action and change.
Quirks: Constantly adjusts her camera, even when unnecessary. Brushes her hair out of her face when deep in thought.
Mannerisms: Frequently quotes films to emphasize her points. Keeps a battered electronic notebook for jotting ideas.
Personality: Passionate and detail-oriented, Alvida strives for perfection in her work and challenges others to meet her high standards.

Sophie *Tech Entrepreneur with Boundless Energy*
Age: Mid-20s
Appearance: Blonde hair, blue eyes, dressed in black jeans and shirts, often paired with vibrant scarves.
Backstory: The child of two scientists, Sophie's love for experimentation led to a failed startup that taught her resilience. Now focused on quantum technology, she merges science with storytelling to tackle real-world problems.
Quirks: Taps fingers when brainstorming. Claims her colorful scarves "make data less dull." **Mannerisms:** Speaks quickly when excited, often sketching diagrams mid-conversation.
Personality: Inquisitive, optimistic, and tenacious, Sophie is the team's energy source, constantly pushing boundaries and embracing challenges.

Conclusion

In this book, we've explored the seven antenarrative processes developed by David Boje and learned how to apply them to our entrepreneurial journeys. We've seen how David Boje and his fictional characters: Avida, Hilda, and Sofie have used these processes to craft compelling narratives and achieve their goals. By applying these processes to our own stories, we can create a powerful narrative that resonates with our audience and drives business results.

Introduction to Entrepreneur's Storytelling Journey

Integrating Principles and Processes

In this introduction, we'll stitch together the seven True Storytelling® Principles with the seven 'Antenarrative Processes presented in the *anteroom*, and apply them to the Entrepreneur's Storytelling Journey:

Integrating True Storytelling® Principles and Antenarrative Processes

1. Combine Truth and Beneath: Be authentic by aligning What's True by Tapping into your deeply held Passions and Values.
2. Merge Make Room with Before: Respecting Stories Already There by Understanding Historical and Cultural Contexts.
3. Align the Plot with Bets on the Future: Create clear, purposeful Plots by Making Bets on the Future.
4. Connect Timing and Being: Living Stories with Timing by actively Shaping their spacetimemattering.
5. Help Stories Along with Becoming: Helping Stories Along by Restorying Your Little Wow Moments into a New Story.
6. Staging with artifacts and scenes to Communicate to the Four Who's.
7. Reflecting Meets Beyond: Reflecting: How Stories Create Value by Exploring What's Beyond the Status Quo.

Then, we will compare American and Danish storytelling by developing scenes of Conversational Storytelling (Boje & Rosile) between David and American and his fantasy Danish characters: Alvida, Sophie, and Hilda.

Conversational Storytelling Script

(The first scene is set in a cozy, modern training room in Copenhagen. Alvida, a Danish actress, is seated across from David Boje, an American professor, at a wooden table. Alvida is dressed in a stylish outfit, while David is wearing a yellow shirt and black jeans. They are surrounded by whiteboards, markers, and a projector screen.)

Alvida: (smiling) David, I'm excited to learn about your antenarrative process storytelling approach. I've heard great things about it.

David: (smiling back) Thank you, Alvida. I'm looking forward to sharing it with you. But first, I'd like to learn more about Kvikmyter storytelling, the traditional Danish approach. Can you tell me more about it? It's not a good idea to share lists. People remember stories, not lists.

Alvida: (nodding) Of course. Kvikmyter storytelling is a unique blend of oral tradition, folk tales, and personal experiences. It's a way of sharing stories that are deeply rooted in Danish culture.

David: (intrigued) That sounds fascinating. Can you demonstrate it for me?

Alvida: (smiling) I'd be happy to. (pulls out a small notebook and begins to tell a story in a warm, engaging tone)

"Once upon a time, in a small village in Denmark, there was a young girl named Sofie. Sofie loved to explore the woods and meadows around her village, and one day she stumbled upon a hidden glade. In the center of the glade stood an ancient tree, its branches twisted and gnarled with age. Sofie felt drawn to the tree as if it had a secret. She reached out and touched the trunk, and suddenly she was transported to a different time and place. She saw her ancestors, who had lived in the village for generations, working together to build a new home. She saw the struggles they faced, the triumphs they achieved, and the love they shared. And when she returned to the present, she felt a deep connection to her heritage and her community."

David: (impressed) Wow, that's beautiful. I can see why Kvikmyter storytelling is so important in Danish culture.

Alvida: (smiling) Thank you. It's a way of sharing our history, our values, and our experiences with each other.

David: (nodding) I can see the parallels between Kvikmyter storytelling and my antenarrative process storytelling approach. Both involve sharing personal experiences and connecting with others on a deeper level.

Alvida: (curious) Tell me more about your approach. How does it work?

David: (pulling out a whiteboard marker) Well, my approach is based on the seven antenarrative processes: Beneath, Before, Bets, Being, Becoming, Between, and Beyond. Each process represents a different stage in the entrepreneurial journey, from the foundation of the business to its growth and evolution.

Alvida: (intrigued) That sounds fascinating. Can you demonstrate it for me?

David: (smiling) Of course. (begins to draw a diagram on the whiteboard) "Let's say we're talking about a startup that's just getting off the ground. The Beneath process would represent the foundation of the business, the values, and the principles that guide it. The Before process would represent the entrepreneur's past experiences and skills that led them to start the business. The Bets process would represent the calculated risks they take to grow the business. And so on."

Alvida: (impressed) I see. It's a very structured approach, but it also seems very flexible and adaptable.

David: (nodding) Exactly. The antenarrative process storytelling approach is designed to be flexible and adaptable so that entrepreneurs can use it to tell their unique stories and connect with others on a deeper level.

Alvida: (smiling) I think I understand now. Thank you for sharing your approach with me,

David. I'm excited to learn more about it and incorporate it into my storytelling training.

David: (smiling back) The pleasure is mine, Alvida. I'm excited to learn more about Kvikmyter storytelling and how it can be used to connect with others on a deeper level.
(They both nod, and the scene fades to black.)

Danish and American storytelling traditions offer rich examples that can be applied to David Boje's book "The Entrepreneur's Storytelling Journey." Here are practical examples from both cultures:

Danish Storytelling

Hans Christian Andersen, Denmark's most famous storyteller, provides an excellent example of Danish storytelling. His fairy tale "The Ugly Duckling" can be seen as a metaphor for entrepreneurship: "It doesn't matter about being born in a duck yard, as long as you are hatched from a swan's egg." This quote reflects the "Becoming" process in Boje's antenarrative approach, emphasizing transformation and potential.

Another Danish storytelling tradition is the concept of "hygge," which emphasizes coziness and connection. This aligns with the "Between" process in Boje's approach, focusing on relationships and community building.

Hygge" is associated with creating a warm atmosphere, enjoying simple pleasures with loved ones, and being present now, asserting a sense of well-being and comfort in everyday life. It's not strictly a storytelling tradition, but rather a lifestyle h deeply ingrained in Danish culture that we all can learn from. All Lykke, co-founder of Endomondo and former CEO, exemplifies the power of storytelling in entrepreneurship. Her journey from journalist to successful tech entrepreneur resonates with Boje's emphasis on narrative transformation. Lykke once said, "I traded a comfortable position for the risks of entrepreneurship"7. This quote illustrates the entrepreneurial spirit and risk-taking that Boje often discusses in his work.

Another Danish storyteller, Carriene Rendbo, founder of I Love Natural Hair, demonstrates the importance of personal narrative in business. She shares, "Because I struggled with it, I knew others were struggling too. Going natural was very liberating!"3 This aligns with Boje's concept of using personal experiences to connect with customers and build a brand.

Implications for Entrepreneur's Storytelling Journey
These examples demonstrate key themes in Boje's "The Entrepreneur's Storytelling Journey":
1. Transformation narratives: Lykke and Rendbo's stories show how personal transformation can become a powerful business narrative.
2. Resilience and learning: Corcoran's quote aligns with Boje's emphasis on viewing failures as 'steppingstones' to success.
3. Authenticity: Sullivan's advice echoes Boje's focus on authentic storytelling in entrepreneurship.
4. Personal connection: Rendbo's approach demonstrates how personal struggles can be turned into business opportunities, a concept that I often explore.

The storytellers, through their experiences and quotes, provide practical examples of how entrepreneurs can effectively use storytelling to build their businesses and connect with their audiences, reinforcing the concepts presented in this book.

American Storytelling

Steve Jobs, an American entrepreneur and storyteller, often used personal anecdotes to inspire others. His Stanford commencement speech provides a great example:

"You can't connect the dots looking forward; you can only connect them looking backward. So, you have to trust that the dots will somehow connect in your future."

This quote aligns with Boje's "Before" and "Bets" processes, emphasizing past experiences and future risks.

Walt Disney, another American storyteller and entrepreneur, often said:

"If you can dream it, you can do it." This quote embodies the "Beyond" process in Boje's approach, encouraging visionary thinking and future possibilities.

Barbara Corcoran, founder of The Corcoran Group, offers a perspective that aligns with Boje's ideas on resilience and learning from failure. She states, "My best successes came on the heels of failures". This quote emphasizes the iterative nature of entrepreneurship that Boje often discusses in his work.

Kat Sullivan, founder of Marketing Solved & TASSI, provides insight into the importance of self-trust in entrepreneurial storytelling. She advises, "Stop telling yourself you don't know what to do. Yes, you do. Listen to your intuition and trust yourself". This aligns with Boje's emphasis on authenticity in entrepreneurial narratives.

These examples demonstrate how both Danish and American storytelling traditions can provide valuable insights for entrepreneurs, aligning with Boje's antenarrative processes and enhancing the storytelling journey.

We turn next to chapters on the seven antenarrative processes, beginning with beneath.

Chapter 1: " Be authentic by aligning What's True by Tapping into your deeply held passions and values"

Alvida and David explore the Beneath process, learning how to establish their values and first True Storytelling Principle as entrepreneurs.

Combine Truth and Beneath: Be authentic by aligning your entrepreneur story with deeply held values, passions, and assumptions.

(The scene is set outdoors, in front of a cozy cafe in Copenhagen full of Hygge, one flower on the table, a small candle, and mood music. Bicycles of all types, one a whole family, mom, dad, and two kids and presents, whizzing by. Alvida, a Danish actress, is seated across from David Boje, an American professor. Alvida is dressed in a stylish winter outfit, while David is wearing a yellow shirt and black jeans, shivering from the cold. It's snowing. The café owner brings him a blanket and a hot chocolate to drink. They are on a busy boulevard; you can hear the cars.)

Alvida: "In Danish storytelling. We Danes call it Kvikmyter storytelling. We often start with the foundation of our story, which is the Beneath process. This is where we establish our values and principles, and it's essential for creating a strong narrative."

David: "I've been exploring my own Beneath process, and it's been a fascinating journey. As a storytelling coach to entrepreneurs, I've always been focused on helping my clients craft compelling narratives. But recently, I discovered that I have Danish ancestry, and it's changed my perspective on storytelling and entrepreneurship."

Alvida: "That's fascinating, David. Can you tell us more about your discovery and how it's impacted your work as a storytelling coach?"

David: "Yes, of course. When I discovered my Danish ancestry, I began to explore the cultural and historical context of my heritage. I learned about the values and principles that were passed down through generations of Danish storytellers, and it's had a profound impact on my work as a storytelling coach."

As they began by exploring the Beneath process, they quickly realized that it wasn't as easy as they had thought. They had to confront their own biases and assumptions, and they had to be willing to be vulnerable and authentic.

"I'm not sure I'm comfortable with this," Alvida said, her voice laced with uncertainty. "I mean, what if I'm not good enough? What if I'm not worthy of being an entrepreneur?"

David reached out and placed a reassuring hand on her arm. "You are worthy, Alvida. And I'm here to support you every step of the way. We'll figure this out together. Let's do an exercise in Going Beneath."

To make this kind of image for you. Write a brief description of what you look like, your age, and who you will give this introduction to. **Then put that in Grok AI.** https://x.com/i/grok

Let's use storytelling to introduce yourself. Please keep it to one or two minutes. Let's focus on 'Gong Beneath'. In the book I wrote, The Entrepreneur's Storytelling Journey, the Beneath process is all about finding the foundation of our pre-story, where we establish our values and passions, which I call 'emotional authenticity.'.

Write a 1,000 or 2,000-word introduction that focuses on YOU GOING BEYOND. Then put that in https://x.com/i/grok **after this question:** *What narrative elements collectively make Boje's 50-word introduction informative but also engaging, illustrative, and emotionally resonant, embodying the essence of storytelling he advocates for in his coaching?*

For example, my name is David Boje. I am a storytelling coach to entrepreneurs. But that doesn't tell you much. So, take your long introduction and ask Grok AI **to split it into versions that are Going Beneath, 50-words, 100-words, and 200-words.**

I'll start. I will reveal the specific narrative elements that demonstrate GOING BENEATH. Then, I will show you how you can use two Ais for free to rewrite your introduction until you have one that works well for you.

Try Grok AI. https://x.com/i/grok **and then try Perplexity AI. https://www.perplexity.ai/ for contrast.**

After writing a long introduction of one or two thousand words, that is now concise in 50, 100, and a 200-word introduction that you can now use in different contexts to ask AI an important question.

Frame the Question this way: *What narrative elements collectively make Boje's 50-word introduction informative but also engaging, illustrative, and emotionally resonant, embodying the essence of storytelling he advocates for in his coaching?*

50-Word Version:

"I'm David Boje, a storytelling coach. At 53, I discovered my Danish roots, learning the power of emotional authenticity. My 'Beneath' process helps entrepreneurs uncover their true selves, crafting stories that resonate deeply, transforming business narratives into authentic journeys that connect beyond the surface."

David Boje's 50-word introduction embodies the essence of storytelling through *seven* key narrative elements:

1. **Personal Revelation**: By mentioning his discovery of Danish roots at 53, Boje introduces a personal narrative that is both intriguing and relatable, providing a backstory that adds depth to his character and ethos.
2. **Cultural Tie**: The reference to "Danish roots" connects his personal story to a broader cultural narrative, suggesting a rich tradition of storytelling that informs his methodology.
3. **Emotional Authenticity**: This concept is central to his narrative, serving as both the theme and the promise of his coaching. It invites the audience to engage with stories on an emotional level.
4. **Metaphorical Language**: The 'Beneath' process is a metaphor for digging deeper into one's identity, which not only explains his method but does so in a way that's memorable and illustrative.
5. **Transformation Narrative**: By talking about transforming "business narratives into authentic journeys," he frames his work as a journey of change, a classic storytelling trope that implies growth and development.
6. **Connection and Resonance**: The promise of stories that "resonate deeply" speaks directly to the audience's desire for meaningful interaction, suggesting his stories are not just heard but felt.
7. **Conciseness**: Despite the brevity, each word is chosen for its narrative weight, making the introduction both informative and engaging without overwhelming the reader.

These elements collectively craft an introduction that not only informs about what Boje does but also engages the reader by painting a picture of a transformative, emotionally rich storytelling experience, embodying the very principles he teaches.

What narrative elements collectively make Boje's 100-word introduction informative but also engaging, illustrative, and emotionally resonant, embodying the essence of storytelling he advocates for in his coaching?

100-Word Version:

"Hello, I'm David Boje, a storytelling coach. At 53, I found out I was half Danish, which led me to the heart of Danish storytelling, emphasizing emotional authenticity. This discovery shaped my 'Beneath' process, where we delve into the core values and passions that define us. It's about going beyond business to reveal our genuine selves and embracing vulnerability. Inspired by a Danish actress, Alvida, I guide entrepreneurs to find their authentic thunderbolts, crafting narratives that resonate with emotion and build trust. This journey helps clients find their voice, leading to compelling stories and entrepreneurial success."

David Boje's 100-word attains more depth of the Beneath and adds the Outcome Promise. The introduction employs *nine* narrative elements that make it informative, engaging, illustrative, and emotionally resonant, embodying his philosophy of storytelling, but not as concise:

1. Personal Journey: Starting with his discovery of his Danish heritage at 53, Boje presents his own life as a narrative arc, which is both engaging and relatable. This personal touch humanizes him and sets the tone for his coaching approach.
2. Cultural Connection: The mention of Danish storytelling traditions not only informs but also adds a layer of exoticism and depth, suggesting a rich, authentic storytelling heritage that enriches his method.
3. Emotional Authenticity: By repeatedly emphasizing "emotional authenticity," Boje highlights the core of his coaching, which is to connect deeply with one's emotions and authenticity, a theme that resonates emotionally with readers.
4. Metaphorical Depth: The 'Beneath' process and 'authentic thunderbolts' are potent metaphors that memorably illustrate his method. These metaphors convey complexity and depth in understanding oneself, making the narrative illustrative.

5. **Character Inspiration**: Alvida, the Danish actress, adds a narrative character that serves as an inspiration, offering a concrete example of how storytelling can influence personal growth and emotional expression.
6. **Transformation Theme**: The idea of going "beyond business" to "reveal our genuine selves" and "embracing vulnerability" speaks to a transformation narrative, a classic story structure where characters evolve, which here applies to his clients.
7. **Active Engagement**: Phrases like "guide entrepreneurs to find" and "helps clients find their voice" suggest an active, participatory journey, which is engaging as it invites the audience to imagine themselves in this narrative of self-discovery and success.
8. **Outcome Promise**: The introduction promises "compelling stories and entrepreneurial success," which is both informative (about the results of his coaching) and emotionally resonant, as it connects to the aspirations of the audience.
9. **Emotional and Trust Building**: The focus on narratives that "resonate with emotion" and "build trust" directly addresses the emotional needs of storytelling, making the introduction not just informative but also deeply engaging on an emotional level.

What narrative elements collectively make Boje's 200-word introduction informative but also engaging, illustrative, and emotionally resonant, embodying the essence of storytelling he advocates for in his coaching?

200-Word Version:

"Hello, I'm David Boje, a storytelling coach for entrepreneurs. When I turned 53, I discovered my Danish heritage, which opened my eyes to the profound role of emotion in storytelling. Unlike my Scottish mother's stoic nature, Danish culture taught me the value of emotional authenticity, which I now integrate into my coaching through the 'Beneath' process. This process is about exploring the depths beneath the surface of business, uncovering the authentic values and passions that guide us. It's a journey of vulnerability, much like Alvida, a Danish actress from my writings, suggested with her metaphor of thunderbolts - each one representing an aspect of our emotional authenticity. I've thrown my thunderbolts; one bold and assertive, hitting my heart, another wobbly yet finding its way to others' hearts. This pre-story approach, though not fully formed, has been pivotal in my teaching, earning me six consecutive 'Teacher of the Year' awards at Loyola Marymount University, where I showed my students the power of emotional authenticity. For my clients, I guide them through this Beneath process, helping them to weave personal heritage, values, and emotions into stories that forge deep connections, build trust, and move beyond mere transactions to create transformational narratives. Let's embark on this journey together to craft your unique, compelling story."

How does David Boje's 200-word introduction leverage *ten* narrative elements to be informative, engaging, illustrative, and emotionally resonant? Notice it adds the elements of Achievement and Proof of the Call to Action, and the 10th element of reaching a Broad Audience:

1. ***Personal Narrative***: Boje shares his personal story of discovering his Danish heritage at 53, providing a relatable entry point for the reader. This personal touch establishes credibility and relatability, key elements in storytelling.
2. ***Cultural Contrast***: The juxtaposition of his Scottish and Danish backgrounds not only informs about his cultural influences but also sets up a narrative of cultural discovery and synthesis, enriching the story with diverse emotional textures.
3. ***Emotional Authenticity***: This theme is woven throughout, acting as both the subject and the method of his coaching. It's an emotionally resonant concept that speaks to the heart of human connection, making the introduction engaging.
4. ***Metaphorical Language***: The 'Beneath' process and the "thunderbolt" metaphor are vivid, illustrative elements that simplify complex ideas into understandable, memorable images. They serve to engage the imagination of the reader, illustrating his method's depth and impact.
5. ***Character and Anecdote***: Using Alvida, the Danish actress, as a narrative character adds depth, providing a real-world example of how

his storytelling principles work. This also humanizes the concept, making it more engaging.
6. **Transformation and Journey**: The narrative of a "journey of vulnerability" and the promise of "transformational narratives" frames his coaching as a personal odyssey. This narrative arc suggests growth and change, which are inherently engaging and inspirational elements in storytelling.
7. **Achievement and Proof**: Mentioning the 'Teacher of the Year' awards provides concrete evidence of his success, informing the reader about his expertise while also serving as a narrative climax that underscores the effectiveness of his methods.
8. **Interactive Call to Action**: The invitation to "embark on this journey together" is a narrative hook, pulling the reader into the story as a participant rather than just an observer, fostering engagement.
9. **Emotional Connection**: Phrases like "hitting my heart" and "finding its way to others' hearts" directly appeal to emotion, making the introduction resonate on a personal level. The focus on building trust and moving beyond transactions speaks to the emotional needs of storytelling.
10. **Inclusivity and Universality**: By talking about weaving "personal heritage, values, and emotions," Boje taps into universal human experiences, making the narrative inclusive and emotionally accessible to a broad audience.

These elements collectively create a rich tapestry that not only informs about Boje's coaching but also engages the reader through vivid imagery, emotional depth, and a compelling narrative structure, embodying the very storytelling techniques he advocates.

Here is an exercise you can use to GO BENEATH.

Let's embark together on this quest to find your unique story, one that will not only compel but also connect, moving from the surface to the heart of what truly matters in your entrepreneurial spirit."

Rewrite your entrepreneur's introduction focusing on narrative elements that collectively make it informative but also engaging, illustrative, and emotionally resonant, embodying the essence of storytelling you manifest in your coaching.

Then Use Grok AI. https://x.com/i/grok

Here is the 256-word introduction I use:
"Hello, I'm David Boje, your guide in the art of entrepreneurial storytelling. At the age of 53, I unearthed my Danish roots, unlocking a world where storytelling is not just a narrative but an emotional journey. This revelation, contrasting with my Scottish mother's reserved demeanor, inspired my 'Beneath' method—a voyage into the soul of your business, where we unearth your deepest values and passions.

Imagine it like this: Beneath the surface of your daily transactions lies a treasure trove of stories waiting to be told. My approach, the 'Beneath' process, is like diving into the depths of the ocean, where each discovery is a thunderbolt of authenticity, echoing the wisdom of Alvida, the Danish actress from my tales.

I've cast my thunderbolts—one bold and direct, striking at my core, another more hesitant, yet with a power that reaches into the hearts of others. This narrative journey, though still evolving, has been the cornerstone of my teaching, earning me six years in a row as 'Teacher of the Year' at Loyola Marymount University, where I've shown my students how stories can transform.

For you, as an entrepreneur, I offer this journey through the 'Beneath' process. It's about weaving the threads of your heritage, your values, and your emotions into narratives that resonate, build trust, and transcend mere business dealings into something truly transformative.

Let's embark together on this quest to find your unique story, one that will not only compel but also connect, moving from the surface to the heart of what truly matters in your entrepreneurial spirit."

David Boje's introduction in this version is crafted with several narrative elements that render it informative, engaging, illustrative, and emotionally resonant, embodying the storytelling essence he promotes:

1. **Personal Narrative**: Boje shares his discovery of Danish heritage at 53, positioning his life experience as the foundation of his coaching philosophy. This personal story adds authenticity and relatability, making the introduction engaging.
2. **Cultural Dichotomy**: The contrast between his Scottish and Danish backgrounds serves as a narrative device to introduce the concept of emotional authenticity versus stoicism, providing depth to his story and method.
3. **Metaphorical Journey**: The 'Beneath' method is described as a "voyage into the soul of your business," using the metaphor of ocean diving to illustrate the depth of introspection and discovery involved. This metaphor makes the process vivid and engaging.
4. **Vivid Imagery and Metaphor**: The use of "thunderbolts" as metaphors for moments of authenticity adds an illustrative, almost mythical quality to the narrative, making complex ideas of emotional resonance tangible and memorable.
5. **Character Reference**: Alvida, the Danish actress, brings in a character from his stories, providing a concrete example of how storytelling can influence personal and professional growth, enhancing the narrative with depth and history.

6. **Transformation and Growth**: The narrative of his teaching success and the transformation of students at Loyola Marymount University serves as proof of concept, informing readers about the efficacy of his methods while also framing his journey as one of growth and achievement.
7. **Interactive Call to Action**: Inviting the reader to "embark together on this quest" actively involves them in the narrative, suggesting a shared journey of discovery, which is both engaging and emotionally appealing.
8. **Emotional Engagement**: Phrases like "striking at my core" and "reaching into the hearts of others" directly speak to the emotional aspect of storytelling, making the introduction resonate on an emotional level.
9. **The theme of Authenticity**: The recurring theme of authenticity, from personal heritage to business values, underscores the emotional and narrative depth Boje aims to achieve, offering a coherent message about the power of genuine storytelling.
10. **Inclusivity in Storytelling**: By weaving together personal heritage, values, and emotions, Boje's narrative suggests that everyone has a story worth telling, which is both informative about his method and emotionally resonant for potential clients.

These elements collectively craft an introduction that not only informs about Boje's coaching but also engages the reader through storytelling techniques that are illustrative, emotionally rich, and deeply connective, embodying the very principles he teaches.

Next, use Perplexity AI. https://www.perplexity.ai
Ask the same question about your introduction. This is the result I obtained:

David Boje's 256-word introduction embodies several key narrative elements that make it informative, engaging, illustrative, and emotionally resonant:

1. **Personal anecdote**: Boje begins with a personal story about discovering his Danish roots at 53, immediately creating a connection with the audience and illustrating the power of storytelling in one's life.
2. **Contrast and comparison**: He juxtaposes his newfound Danish storytelling heritage with his Scottish mother's reserved nature, highlighting the diversity of storytelling approaches1.
3. **Metaphorical language**: Boje uses vivid metaphors like "diving into the depths of the ocean" and "thunderbolts of authenticity" to illustrate his 'Beneath' method, making abstract concepts more tangible and memorable.
4. **Emotional journey**: By sharing his evolution and the emotional impact of his discoveries, Boje demonstrates the transformative power of storytelling.
5. **Credibility building**: Mentioning his "Teacher of the Year" awards establishes his expertise and the effectiveness of his methods.
6. **Audience Engagement**: Boje directly addresses the entrepreneur, inviting them into the narrative and showing how his method applies to their journey.
7. **Sensory details**: The use of vivid imagery and sensory language helps to create a more immersive experience for the listener.
8. **Cultural references**: By mentioning Alvida, the Danish actress, Boje adds depth and authenticity to his narrative, rooting it in a cultural context.
9. **The promise of transformation**: Boje concludes by offering a journey that goes beyond business, promising a transformative experience through storytelling.

These elements collectively create a narrative that not only informs about Boje's method but also engages the audience emotionally, illustrates his concepts vividly, and embodies the very storytelling techniques he advocates for in his coaching.

What do the above examples tell you? Answer: You can pack seven narrative elements into a 50-word introduction, nine into a 100-word introduction, and ten into a 200-word introduction. Each version can be used with different audiences and attain different entrepreneurial storytelling journey objectives.

"Imagine embarking on a journey where your business narrative transforms into something truly authentic and compelling. I'm David Boje, and I've walked this path myself, discovering at 53 that my Danish roots offered me a new lens on storytelling, one rich with emotional authenticity. This revelation not only changed my approach but also led me to develop the 'Beneath' process, which has been the cornerstone of my success as a storytelling coach.

Now let's do some coaching of someone else:
David motioned to Alvida: "Now you try it."

Alvida's 50-Word Introduction:

*The camera focuses on Alvida in a cozy Copenhagen café, the soft light enhancing her expressive eyes. She speaks with heartfelt emotion, "I'm Alvida, a Danish actress turning filmmaker. Through 'Going Beneath,' I dive into my roots to craft authentic stories, helping entrepreneurs tell their tales on YouTube and Facebook."

Alvida's 100-Word Introduction:

*In a warm, intimate Copenhagen café, the camera zooms in on Alvida, her face illuminated by the soft glow of ambient light. With genuine emotion, she begins, "Hello, I am Alvida, a Danish actress embracing the journey of becoming a filmmaker. My practice of 'Going Beneath' has led me to explore my cultural identity deeply, drawing from my rich acting background to bring authenticity to storytelling. I'm here to assist entrepreneurs on their storytelling journey, translating their visions into compelling films for YouTube and Facebook. My passion is to help you resonate with your audience through the lens of genuine emotion."

Alvida's 200-word Introduction:

*The scene opens in a quaint café in Copenhagen, the atmosphere filled with warmth and the scent of freshly brewed coffee. Alvida, with her Danish heritage shining through, stands in the soft light, her voice quivering with genuine emotion as she starts her introduction. "Hej, I'm Alvida, a Danish actress on a transformative path to becoming a filmmaker. My storytelling journey has been profoundly influenced by the 'Going Beneath' process, inspired by David Boje. This practice has allowed me to delve into the depths of my cultural roots, embracing the emotional authenticity that Danish storytelling is known for. With years of acting experience, I've learned to convey deep emotions, a skill I now wish to share with entrepreneurs."

*She pauses, her eyes reflecting a heartfelt connection with her audience. "My mission is to help you on your entrepreneurial storytelling journey by creating films that capture the essence of your business. Whether it's for YouTube or Facebook, I aim to craft narratives that not only showcase your products or services but also tell your personal story, your values, and your passions. Through this cinematic journey, we'll go beneath the surface, finding the authentic self that will resonate with your audience, creating a bond beyond business. Let's weave your story together, with genuine emotion at its core."

As Alvida and David continued to explore the Beneath process, they began to feel a sense of unease and tension between them. They had been working together for weeks, but it seemed like they were at a standstill.

"I don't know if I can do this anymore," Alvida said, her voice laced with frustration. "I feel like we're just going around in circles."

David sighed. "I know what you mean. I feel like we're not making any progress. But I don't know what else to do."

Just then, a figure appeared at the edge of the clearing. It was Hilda, a shaman from Lapland, dressed in traditional clothing and carrying a staff.

"Ah, David and Alvida," she said, her eyes twinkling with wisdom. "I have been watching you from afar. I sense that you are struggling with the Beneath process. Come with me."

Hilda led them to a nearby cave, where she lit a fire and began to chant and dance. The air was filled with the scent of burning sage and the sound of drums.

"This is the spirit of nature," Hilda said, her voice rising and falling with the rhythm of the drums. "It is here that we can find the answers we seek."

As they sat in silence, Alvida and David began to feel a sense of calm wash over them. They closed their eyes and breathed deeply, allowing themselves to let go of their doubts and fears.

Suddenly, Hilda spoke again. "The spirit of nature has a message for you. It says that you must let go of your ego and your fears. You must trust in the process and have faith in yourselves."

As they opened their eyes, Alvida and David looked at each other with newfound understanding. They knew that they had been given a great gift - the gift of clarity and purpose.

"Thank you, Hilda," David said, his voice filled with gratitude. "We will take your words to heart and continue on our journey."

Hilda smiled. "I knew you would. Remember, the Beneath process is not just about finding your values and principles, it's about being willing to share them with the world and use them to guide your decisions and actions."

As they left the cave, Alvida and David felt a sense of peace and resolution. They knew that they had been given a second chance to work together and to find their true purpose.

"I'm glad we did this," Alvida said, her voice filled with emotion. "I feel like we've been given a new lease on life."

David nodded in agreement. "Me too. And I know that we'll be able to overcome any obstacle that comes our way."

As they continued to explore the Beneath process, they began to uncover some surprising insights. They realized that their values and principles were not just about their business, but about who they were as people.

"I never realized how much my person and principles were tied to my business,"

Alvida said, her eyes wide with amazement. "I mean, I always thought I was just a business owner, but it turns out I'm so much more than that."

David smiled. "Exactly. And that's the power of the Beneath process. It's not just about finding your values and principles; it's about being willing to share them with the world and use them to guide your decisions and actions."

David nodded in agreement. "Me too. And I think that's the beauty of the Beneath process. It's not just about finding your values and authenticity; it's about being willing to share them with the world and use them to guide your decisions and actions."

As they stood up to leave, Alvida turned to David and smiled. "You know, I think we make a pretty good team."

David smiled back. "I think you're right. And I'm excited to see where this journey takes us."
And with that, they walked out of the room, ready to face whatever challenges lay ahead, armed with their newfound sense of purpose and direction.

Alvida: "That's amazing. Can you give us some examples of how your discovery has changed your approach to storytelling?"

David: "One example is that I've started to focus more on the emotional connections between the entrepreneur and their audience. In Danish storytelling, emotions are a crucial element, and I've found that by tapping into the emotions of my clients, I can help them craft more compelling narratives that resonate with their audience."

Alvida: "That's a great example, David. And what about the values and principles that guide your work as a storytelling coach? Have you discovered any new values or principles that are important to you?"

David: "Yes, I have. One value that I've discovered is the importance of authenticity. In Danish storytelling, authenticity is key, and I've found that by being authentic and vulnerable in my storytelling, I can build deeper connections with my clients and help them craft more compelling narratives."

Alvida: "That's a great value to have, David. And finally, how do you think the Beneath process has impacted your work as a storytelling coach?"

David: "The Beneath process has been a game-changer for me. By exploring my values and authenticity, I've been able to help my clients do the same, and it's led to more authentic and compelling storytelling. I've also found that by focusing on the emotional connections between the entrepreneur and their audience, I can help them craft narratives that resonate with their audience on a deeper level."

David: "I've also had the pleasure of working with many entrepreneurs, including my wife, Grace Ann Rosile, who is a coach and equine therapist. She uses equine therapy to help her clients discover their values and principles, and it's been incredibly effective. She's also taught me a lot about the importance of authenticity in storytelling."

Alvida: "Yes, authenticity is key in Danish storytelling. As an actress, I've learned that when I'm authentic and vulnerable on stage, I can connect with my audience on a deeper level. And as a coach, I've seen the same thing happen with my clients. When they're authentic and themselves, they're able to craft narratives that resonate with their audience."

David: "I completely agree. As a storytelling coach, I've seen many American entrepreneurs struggle to find their values and principles. They often focus on the surface-level aspects of their business, such as their products or services, and forget to explore what lies beneath them. But when they do, they're able to craft narratives that are authentic and compelling."

Alvida: "That's so true. And it's not just about finding your values and principles, it's also about being willing to share them with your audience. When you're authentic and vulnerable, you're able to build deeper connections with your audience and create a sense of trust and loyalty."

David: "Exactly. And that's why the Beneath process is so important. It's not just about finding your values and authenticity; it's about being willing to share them with your audience and use them to guide your decisions and actions. When you do, you're able to craft narratives that are authentic, compelling, and memorable."

As they finished their exploration of the Beneath process, Alvida and David felt a sense of relief and accomplishment. They had faced their fears and doubts, and they had come out the other side with a newfound sense of purpose and direction.

"I'm so glad we did this," Alvida said, her voice filled with gratitude. "I feel like I have a newfound sense of clarity and purpose. And I know that I can apply this to my business and my personal life."

In this chapter, we've explored the Beneath process, a crucial step in crafting a compelling narrative as an entrepreneur. By establishing our values authentically, we can create a strong foundation for our story and build deeper connections with our audience.

Examples of Entrepreneurs Applying the Beneath Process

1. Anita Roddick, founder of The Body Shop, built her company on principles of ethical sourcing and environmental sustainability.

2. Blake Mycoskie, founder of TOMS Shoes, established a one-for-one giving model based on his value of social responsibility.

3. Yvon Chouinard, founder of Patagonia, created a company culture centered on environmental activism and outdoor preservation.

4. "Your beliefs become your thoughts. Your thoughts become your words. Your words become your actions. Your actions become your habits. Your habits become your values. Your values become your destiny." - Mahatma Gandhi.

5. "Chase the vision, not the money; the money will end up following you." - Tony Hsieh, CEO of Zippo's

6. "How you climb a mountain is more important than reaching the top." - Yvon Chouinard, founder of Patagonia.

7. "My values, our values, aren't about pointing fingers. They are about offering a helping hand." - Kathleen Blanco, Former Governor of Louisiana.

Here are the Main Points about the Beneath Process.

Go Beneath the Surface
The Beneath process involves going deeper than surface-level aspects of a business to uncover the core values and pre-story events that guide an entrepreneur's decisions and actions. This process is essential for:
1. Establishing a strong narrative foundation
2. Uncovering authentic values
3. Creating stories that resonate with audiences
4. Building deeper connections with customers and stakeholders

As entrepreneurs, we often focus on the surface-level aspects of our business, such as our products or services, our marketing strategies, and our financial goals. But what lies beneath the surface? What are the values and principles that guide our decisions and actions?

The Importance of Authenticity
Authenticity emerges as a key value in both Danish storytelling and entrepreneurial narratives. By being genuine and vulnerable, entrepreneurs can forge stronger connections with their audience. This approach allows for the creation of stories that not only captivate listeners but also build trust and loyalty.

Emotional Connections
Danish storytelling traditions emphasize the significance of emotional connections. By tapping into the emotions of both the storyteller and the audience, entrepreneurs can craft narratives that resonate more profoundly[6]. This emotional

resonance is crucial for creating memorable and impactful stories that stand out in a crowded marketplace.

Cultural Context and Heritage

David's exploration of his Danish ancestry highlights the importance of understanding one's cultural and historical context. This knowledge can provide valuable insights into storytelling techniques and values that have been passed down through generations[6]. By incorporating these elements, entrepreneurs can add depth and richness to their narratives.

The Beneath Process Practical Applications

Entrepreneurs can apply the Beneath process by:
1. Exploring their personal and cultural heritage
2. Identifying core values that guide their business
3. Incorporating a little vulnerability into their storytelling
4. Focusing on emotional connections with their audience
5. Address customer values to inform business decisions and actions
6. Identify core values that resonate with you and your business vision

By embracing the Beneath process, entrepreneurs can craft narratives that are not only compelling but also true to their core values and principles. This approach leads to more authentic storytelling and stronger connections with audiences, ultimately contributing to entrepreneurial success.

By incorporating these tips, examples, and quotes into their Beneath process, Alvida and David are coaches who can develop a strong foundation of values and principles to guide their entrepreneurial journey. This foundation will not only shape their business decisions but also help them craft authentic and compelling narratives that resonate with their audience.

Chapter 2: "Respect Stories Already There by Understanding Historical and Cultural Contexts"

Storytelling is the flame of entrepreneurship. Entrepreneurs craft and share the fire of pre-stories to engage stakeholders, build trust, and inspire action. In this book, The Entrepreneur's Storytelling Journey: Seven Antenarrative Processes for Success (2024), I intend to provide you with a framework for creating compelling entrepreneurial narratives using the antenarrative processes. These processes—Beneath, Before, Bets, Being, Becoming, Between, and Beyond—offer entrepreneurs a transformative lens for understanding their journey, connecting with their audience, and envisioning the future. Here we focus on the BEFORE.

Keeping the Flame of the BEFORE Alive

SCENE 1: DAVID'S CHILDHOOD WORKSHOP
The camera pans over a cluttered workshop filled with tools, wood shavings, and jars of nails. A young DAVID (12) watches his grandfather, AUGUST BOJE, meticulously craft a stained-glass window.

AUGUST: (smiling) David, you see these colors? Every piece has a story. If you don't arrange them just right, the window won't shine.

YOUNG DAVID: (curious) But what if the glass breaks?

AUGUST: Then you pick up the pieces and start again. That's what being a craftsman—and an entrepreneur—is about.

David watches, fascinated, as August holds a piece of glass up to the light.

SCENE 2: CONVERSATION WITH ALVIDA
Present-day. David sits across from ALVIDA, a Danish filmmaker, in his workshop. She holds a camera, documenting his stories.

ALVIDA: Your grandfather's workshop—do you think that's where your flame started?

DAVID: (nodding) Definitely. It was there I learned every piece has a story. That idea stayed with me—even in Vietnam, building a driving range in the middle of a war zone.

ALVIDA: (smiling) Resilience. That's what makes a great story.

SCENE 3: VIETNAM (1968)
David, now in his 20s, stands on a dusty field, hammering a post into the ground. A Navy officer approaches.

NAVY OFFICER: What's this, soldier?

DAVID: (wiping sweat) A driving range. Generals need practice too, right?

NAVY OFFICER: (laughing) You're a hustler, Boje.

David steps back, admiring the makeshift golf range.

DAVID (V.O.): Even there, my flame stayed alive.

SCENE 4: DISCUSSION WITH HILDA
David meets with HILDA, a shaman, at a storytelling circle. They sit by a fire under a starry sky.

HILDA: The Blackfeet believe a flame is a sacred guide. It burns brighter when you honor it.

DAVID: (thoughtful) That's how I see my pre-stories. They're not just memories—they're fuel.

HILDA: And when others try to put it out?

DAVID: (smiling) You tend the fire. Keep it alive.

SCENE 5: SOPHIE'S MASTERCLASS DEVELOPMENT
SOPHIE sits with David in his office, brainstorming for her masterclass.

SOPHIE: The BEFORE—it's brilliant. But how do we teach people to keep their flame alive?

DAVID: (leaning forward) Show them how failure is part of the story. My dad failed a hundred times to perfect his trash compactor. Each failure fed the flame.

SOPHIE: (writing) Failure as fuel. Got it.

SCENE 6: THE AI COLLABORATION WITH QUARK
David works with QUARK, a sleek AI hologram, in his workshop. Quark displays holographic diagrams of pre-stories.

QUARK: Analysis suggests your audience connects most with stories of perseverance. Shall I highlight those?

DAVID: (chuckling) Smart robot. Yes, Quark. Let's make those stories shine.

QUARK: A brighter flame, Professor Boje. Always brighter.

SCENE 7: THE BEFORE PROCESS IS BORN (2000)
David, now a professor, stands in front of a whiteboard with "The BEFORE" written across it. A group of students listens intently.

DAVID: (gesturing) The Before isn't just about the past. It's about the pre-stories—the fragments that shape who we are and where we're going.

STUDENT: (raising hand) But what if we fail?

DAVID: Failure is part of the story. My dad taught me that. Every failure is a piece of the puzzle.

SCENE 8: MASTERCLASS INTRODUCTION
David stands on a brightly lit stage, speaking to a room full of aspiring entrepreneurs.

DAVID: (to the audience) Your story begins in the Before. It's messy, full of failures and small victories. But it's where your greatest ideas are born.

SOPHIE: (in the audience, smiling) Fuel for the flame.

CLOSING SCENE
David closes his laptop and steps outside into the sunlight. He joins ALVIDA, HILDA, SOPHIE, and QUARK in the yard of his workshop. They discuss his stories, the flame burning brightly in their conversations.

DAVID (V.O.): The flame of creativity burns in all of us. Tend it, nurture it, and let it guide you to new histories.

FADE OUT.

TITLE CARD:
"The Secrets of the BEFORE: A Journey of Creativity, Resilience, and Innovation"

PRACTICAL TIPS FOR ENTREPRENEURS - APPLYING THE BEFORE PROCESS

David gestures to the whiteboard, where he writes five key points. Each point is accompanied by commentary from the participants.

1. **Reflect on Your Past Experiences**
   DAVID: Identify your pivotal moments—successes, failures, lessons.

   ALVIDA: For me, it's when my first film flopped. That failure taught me resilience and authenticity.

   SOPHIE: My startup almost collapsed, but it forced me to innovate faster.

2. **Identify Your Values and Passions**
   DAVID: Your values are your compass. Find what drives you.

   HILDA: My values come from the Earth—connection, respect, and balance. They guide everything I do.

3. **Connect with Your Audience**
   DAVID: Understand your audience. Empathy is key.

   QUARK: (processing data) Audience analysis reveals that shared values enhance engagement by 73%.

   DAVID: (chuckling) Thanks for the stats, Quark.

4. **Use Storytelling to Share Your Experience**
   DAVID: Frame your journey as a story. Highlight struggles, growth, and triumphs.

   ALVIDA: Storytelling isn't just an art—it's a bridge between people.

5. **Turn Setbacks into Stepping Stones**
   DAVID: Reframe failures as opportunities.

   SOPHIE: Setbacks are where creativity thrives. It's where quantum possibilities emerge.

WORKSHOP DISCUSSION

The group buzzes with energy. Alvida scribbles notes furiously. Quark processes data, displaying holograms of key points. Sophie brainstorms on her tablet, while Hilda reflects with quiet wisdom.

DAVID: Remember, the Before isn't about clinging to the past. It's about learning from it, reshaping it, and using it to propel your future.

CLOSING SHOT

David smiles as the participants share their insights. The camera pans out, showing the workshop filled with ideas, energy, and connection.

DAVID (V.O.): Your story doesn't start today. It began long ago, in the Before. Now it's up to you to make it extraordinary.

FADE OUT.

ON-SCREEN QUOTE:
"The Before is your foundation—use it to build something extraordinary."

End of Chapter 2: The Antenarrative Called the Before

STUDY GUIDE: Introduction of you the Entrepreneur exploring the BEFORE of multiple simultaneous histories.

Here are my examples in introducing the BEFORE.

50-Word Introduction

I'm David Boje, creator of the BEFORE process, which nurtures the pre-stories shaping entrepreneurial journeys. My creative flame ignited early—crafting sculptures in art class and impressing an instructor by making lasting designs with fiberglass. Though critics often tried to extinguish it, I persisted, turning small sparks into transformative bonfires.

David Boje's 50-word introduction embodies several narrative elements that make it both informative and emotionally engaging, resonating with his goal of keeping the entrepreneurial flame alive:

1. Personal Narrative

- Boje shares a vivid memory of his early creative achievements, grounding his authority in personal experience.
  Effect: Builds authenticity and relatability, engaging the audience with a real-life example.

2. Transformation and Growth

- The narrative moves from a small creative spark in art class to Boje transforming setbacks into impactful results.
  Effect: Inspires entrepreneurs to see how persistence can turn initial ideas into meaningful successes.

3. Emotional Engagement

- Phrases like "critics tried to extinguish it" and "turning small sparks into transformative bonfires" evoke resilience and determination.
  Effect: Resonates emotionally, motivating the audience to nurture their creative flame despite challenges.

4. Metaphor and Imagery

- The metaphor of "small sparks" becoming "bonfires" illustrates growth and innovation tangibly and memorably Making the abstract idea of nurturing pre-stories more vivid and actionable.

5. Call to Action (Implied)

- By framing his journey as an example, Boje implicitly invites entrepreneurs to reflect on their own pre-stories and creative potential. **Effect**: Encourages enrollment in his masterclass by positioning the BEFORE as a tool for transformation.

Conclusion

Boje's introduction weaves personal history, resilience, and vivid imagery into a compact, emotionally resonant narrative. It reflects the essence of his masterclass, inspiring entrepreneurs to uncover, nurture, and ignite their transformed journeys.

100-Word Introduction

Hello, I'm David Boje, and I developed the BEFORE process to help entrepreneurs nurture the pre-stories that fuel innovation. My journey began in workshops, like crafting sculptures with fiberglass after an instructor dismissed their longevity. This creative spark stayed with me, even as rejections and academic constraints tried to dim it.

In Vietnam, I stoked the flame further, bartering materials to construct a golf driving range in a war zone, learning resilience and resourcefulness. My flame burned brighter despite critics, enabling me to publish *The Entrepreneur's Storytelling Journey*. Today, I help others turn their pre-story sparks into transformative ventures.

David Boje's 100-word introduction incorporates multiple narrative elements that make it informative, engaging, illustrative, and emotionally resonant. These elements collectively reflect the essence of his masterclass, *The Secrets of the BEFORE*, and inspire entrepreneurs to enroll:

1. Personal Narrative

- Boje shares pivotal moments in his life—crafting sculptures, overcoming rejection, and innovating under pressure in Vietnam.
  Effect: Makes the introduction relatable and credible, showing that his teachings are grounded in real experiences.

2. Transformation and Growth

- From dismissed sculptures to building a golf driving range in a war zone, Boje demonstrates how creativity and resilience lead to breakthroughs.
  Effect: Encourages entrepreneurs to see challenges as opportunities to strengthen their flame and innovate.

3. Emotional Engagement

- The imagery of "rejections and constraints dimming the flame" and "sparks into transformative ventures" evokes determination and hope.
  Effect: Resonates deeply, motivating readers to protect and nurture their creative flame.

4. Vivid Metaphor

- The flame symbolizes creativity and perseverance, giving a tangible and inspirational representation of the entrepreneurial journey.
  Effect: Makes abstract concepts memorable and engaging.

5. Call to Action (Implied)

- Boje's journey frames his masterclass as a guide to turning sparks into success.
  Effect: Positions his masterclass as essential for those seeking resilience and innovation.

Conclusion

This introduction weaves Boje's personal experiences with a powerful call to action, embodying the transformative essence of the BEFORE process.

250-Word Introduction

I'm David Boje, and I created the BEFORE process—a framework that nurtures the pre-stories shaping entrepreneurship. My creative flame started early, fueled by hands-on experiences. In art class, I ignored my instructor's advice to dismantle temporary sculptures, using fiberglass to craft something enduring. That spark taught me to defy limits and innovate.

In Vietnam, I built a driving range in a war zone, hustling for materials and showcasing creativity under pressure. Back home, I watched my father's inventive flame as he reworked failed designs for a trash compactor, proving perseverance ignites breakthroughs, while academia tried to extinguish my voice. Critics dismissed my unconventional ideas, urging me to stop writing. Rejections piled up, but I kept feeding my flame—learning from failures, embracing pre-stories, and turning fragments of ideas into published works. My persistence led to *The Entrepreneur's Storytelling Journey* and collaborative sci-fi novels with the "Enthinkment Circle."

Your flame is your pre-story—a living aliveness that resists extinguishment. It may face dampening forces: critics, failures, and doubt. But when nurtured, it can light paths to new histories and ventures. My masterclass teaches how to uncover and protect that flame, helping entrepreneurs craft narratives that transform ideas into realities.

Let's keep your flame alive, burn brighter, and inspire a future only you can create.

David Boje's 250-word introduction effectively combines several narrative elements that make it informative, engaging, illustrative, and emotionally resonant. Together, these elements embody the essence of his *BEFORE* process, inspiring entrepreneurs to enroll in his masterclass:

1. Personal Narrative

- Boje shares formative experiences, from art class defiance to his father's perseverance, grounding the *BEFOR E*piocess in life.
  Effect: Adds authenticity and relatability, demonstrating that the framework is rooted in lived experiences.

2. Transformation and Growth

- The narrative transitions from early sparks of creativity to breakthroughs achieved through resilience.
  Effect: Inspires entrepreneurs to see challenges as transformative opportunities, aligning with the flame metaphor.

3. Emotional Engagement

- Phrases like "critics dismissed my ideas" and "rejections piled up" evoke empathy, while the "living aliveness" of the flame inspires hope.
  Effect: Establish a connection with readers who may also face obstacles, motivating them to keep their flames alive.

4. Metaphorical Imagery

- The flame metaphor ties the narrative together, representing creativity, perseverance, and growth.
  Effect: Creates a vivid, memorable framework that illustrates the emotional core of entrepreneurship.

5. Call to Action

- By linking his experiences to the masterclass, Boje invites readers to uncover and protect their creative flame.
  Effect: The *BEFORE* process is essential for crafting transformative narratives and realizing entrepreneurial potential.

Conclusion

This introduction blends personal storytelling with vivid imagery and a compelling call to action, showcasing the transformative power of the *BEFORE* process while resonating deeply with entrepreneurial audiences.

52

How Time Dilation and Time Curvature Influence David Boje's Before Process

Time dilation, rooted in Einstein's theory of relativity, describes how time is perceived differently based on velocity or gravitational forces, creating a curvature in spacetime. While traditionally applied in physics, this concept can metaphorically and practically influence David Boje's *Before process*, which emphasizes multiple, simultaneous histories shaping entrepreneurship.

1. Time is Not Linear in the Before Process

- Boje's Before process already challenges linear notions of time, suggesting that histories are not sequential but exist in a web of interconnected narratives.
- Time dilation deepens this idea, showing that "Before" moments may unfold or be perceived differently depending on one's context or vantage point. Entrepreneurs' perceptions of their pasts might vary due to external factors like cultural, technological, or emotional "gravitational forces."

Impact: Entrepreneurs may see certain pivotal moments as stretched (long-lasting in influence) or compressed (quick but impactful), emphasizing the relativity of how past experiences shape present actions.

2. Multiplicity of Histories and Simultaneity

- Time dilation supports the concept of multiple, simultaneous histories, as it demonstrates that different observers experience time uniquely based on their "frame of reference."
- Similarly, in the Before process, histories are not singular but multifaceted. An event can have different interpretations depending on cultural, technological, or personal perspectives.

Impact: Entrepreneurs are encouraged to embrace this multiplicity, recognizing that their Before is not fixed and may differ from how others view it. This enhances their ability to craft inclusive and empathetic narratives.

3. Expansion of the Before

- Just as time dilation allows for time to stretch under specific conditions, it metaphorically allows the Before process to expand beyond traditional constraints.
- By considering historical moments as "curved" or "stretched," entrepreneurs can integrate broader societal, ecological, or quantum perspectives into their narratives, weaving stories that transcend individual experiences.

Impact: The Before becomes a tool for exploring systemic patterns and collective histories, enabling entrepreneurs to connect their ventures to larger contexts.

4. Nonlinearity and Entrepreneurial Resilience

- Time curvature implies that time loops, overlaps, or folds, challenging the concept of a single start or endpoint. This aligns with Boje's assertion that history is unstable and constantly rewritten.

- Entrepreneurs can revisit and reinterpret their Before, finding new meanings in old experiences.

Impact: Entrepreneurs gain resilience by recognizing that failures or setbacks are not endpoints but part of a cyclical, nonlinear journey.

5. Quantum Implications: Reimagining Time and Possibility

- Quantum theories, such as superposition, suggest that multiple states can coexist until observed, paralleling time dilation's implications for Boje's Before process.
- Entrepreneurs can view their Before as holding multiple potential narratives simultaneously, choosing which to emphasize based on their current needs or vision.

Impact: This approach empowers entrepreneurs to reinterpret their past creatively, transforming challenges into opportunities and shaping their futures dynamically.

Conclusion

Time dilation and curvature enrich David Boje's *Before process* by emphasizing the relativity, multiplicity, and nonlinear nature of time. Entrepreneurs are encouraged to see their histories not as fixed but as dynamic, layered, and open to reinterpretation, enabling them to craft authentic, transformative narratives that resonate deeply with their audience. The metaphors of time dilation and curvature thus reinforce the process's depth and flexibility, making it a powerful tool for navigating entrepreneurial journeys.

The Seven Antenarrative Processes

1. Beneath: Establishing Values and Passions
The Beneath process forms the foundation of an entrepreneurial story. This stage involves uncovering the values, passions, and personal commitments

that drive an entrepreneur's vision. Entrepreneurs often overlook this pre-story layer, but it is here that authenticity is rooted.

Application Example: A social entrepreneur addressing climate change draws upon personal values of sustainability and equity to frame their narrative, inspiring stakeholders who share those values.

2. Before: Context and Past Experiences
The Before process delves into the context in which the story unfolds, incorporating the entrepreneur's past experiences and skills. It recognizes that the origins of a venture are as significant as its outcomes, connecting past learnings to present opportunities.

Historical Pivot Relation: The Renaissance drew from classical antiquity to reshape art, science, and thought. Entrepreneurs, like Renaissance thinkers, can harness their personal histories to inform their ventures.

Practical Tip: Share personal anecdotes about the journey that led to founding the business, creating emotional resonance with audiences.

3. Bets: Calculated Risks and Strategic Decisions
Bets are the calculated risks entrepreneurs take to achieve their goals. This process is about navigating uncertainty and placing strategic "bets" on actions that align with long-term objectives.
- **Boje's Insight:** Storytelling about risks emphasizes courage and resilience, helping entrepreneurs convey determination even when outcomes are uncertain.
- **Example:** A Danish entrepreneur launching a sustainable fashion line uses storytelling to articulate the risks and rewards of ethical production practices.

4. Being: Identity and Sense of Self
Being explores how an entrepreneur's identity and sense of self inform their storytelling and decision-making. Heidegger's concept of "Being in the world" and Kierkegaard's existentialist notions of identity resonates with this antenarrative process.
- **Application:** Entrepreneurs can reflect on how their personal experiences, strengths, and vulnerabilities shape their venture. This authenticity fosters trust and connection.
- **Boje's Perspective:** Storytelling as Being is not just about promoting a brand but embodying the values and aspirations of the entrepreneur.

5. Becoming: Transformation and Growth
The Becoming process focuses on the transformation and growth of the entrepreneur and their venture. It acknowledges the journey of change, learning, and resilience that defines entrepreneurship.
- **Connection to Historical Pivots:** The Industrial Revolution represents societal Becoming, transforming economies and labor systems. Similarly, entrepreneurial Becoming entails adapting and evolving to meet challenges.
- **Example:** A tech startup founder shares stories of early failures and how they shaped the company's eventual success.

6. Between: Building Connections and Relationships
The Between process emphasizes relationality, focusing on the connections entrepreneurs build with customers, stakeholders, and ecosystems. This process acknowledges the interdependence of all entities in an entrepreneurial ecosystem.
- **Boje's Insight:** Storytelling as Between weaves networks of collaboration and mutual support, mirroring the Renaissance's intellectual exchanges.
- **Practical Application:** Entrepreneurs can use storytelling to highlight partnerships, community engagement, and shared goals.

7. Beyond: Vision and Goals for the Future
The Beyond process propels entrepreneurs into uncharted territories, articulating visions and goals that transcend current boundaries. It is a forward-looking narrative that inspires action and innovation.
1. **Boje's Contribution:** By embracing the unknown, storytelling as Beyond aligns with quantum storytelling principles, where possibilities emerge from creative exploration.

Example: A renewable energy entrepreneur shares a bold vision of a fossil-free future, rallying investors and customers around their mission.

Key Takeaways of the Seven Antenarratives for Entrepreneurs:
1. **Understand your Beneath:** Reflect on your foundational values and passions.
2. **Explore your Before:** Draw connections between past experiences and current ventures.
3. **Take thoughtful Bets:** Share stories that demonstrate courage in navigating uncertainty.
4. **Embrace your Being:** Use storytelling to convey authenticity and identity.

5. **Celebrate your Becoming:** Highlight growth and transformation as part of your journey.
6. **Cultivate the Between:** Build meaningful relationships through collaborative narratives.
7. **Envision the Beyond:** Articulate a bold and inspiring vision for the future.

By mastering the art of antenarrative storytelling, entrepreneurs can craft narratives that resonate deeply with their audiences, inspire action, and drive meaningful change.

Chapter 3: "Create clear, purposeful Plots by Making Bets on the Future"

Aligning the Plot with Bets on the Future: Creating Purposeful Narratives that Explore Risks and Opportunities

Introduction: How Entrepreneurs Make Bets on the Future

Entrepreneurship is, at its core, an exercise in betting on the future. It requires vision, courage, and the ability to craft narratives that not only resonate with audiences but also guide bold decision-making. I'm David Boje, and for decades I've explored the art of storytelling in entrepreneurship. I've watched my father, an inventive entrepreneur, make bets on the future that ranged from visionary successes to profound failures. Each story offers lessons on how to align our plots—the narratives we create—with the opportunities and risks of what lies ahead.

The Poker Metaphor: Ante-Up

Entrepreneurial storytelling begins with the willingness to ante up—to commit to a vision. Like playing poker, once you place your money in the pot, it's no longer yours. You've entered the game, and now the story unfolds. Bets on the future are the entrepreneurial equivalent of this commitment. They involve taking calculated risks to pursue a vision, knowing that outcomes are uncertain but guided by a clear plot and narrative.

Learning from My Father's Bets on the Future

My father's entrepreneurial journey was defined by bold bets. After losing his job during a tumultuous time in his life, he invented a trash compactor, betting that it would revolutionize waste management. I vividly remember helping him gather trash from neighborhood buildings for a demonstration. Seventeen white, chauffeur-driven Cadillacs arrived, carrying mayors from across the region. The compactor was loud and messy, but my father convinced them it was the most affordable and effective solution for reducing landfill waste. This longshot bet succeeded, earning him a significant financial windfall.

However, success in one venture does not guarantee success in the next. My father reinvested his earnings into multiple businesses, many of which failed due to unforeseen risks and unreliable partners. From a stock trading house that collapsed to a fraudulent partnership in a coffee maker venture, his stories illustrate the high stakes of entrepreneurial bets. Despite setbacks, his resilience and vision were unwavering, culminating in a patented invention for large-screen TVs. His story underscores the importance of learning from failures and adapting as part of the entrepreneurial journey.

My Entrepreneurial Bets

Like my father, I've placed my share of bets on the future. After leaving academia without tenure, I co-founded a company called Personnel for Printers. We created an algorithm that matched job seekers with employers based on proximity and compatibility, a novel concept at the time. The venture was successful but ultimately led me back to academia, where I made another critical bet: publishing a top-tier journal article to secure tenure at Loyola Marymount University.

Through storytelling-focused teaching, I earned six teaching awards and developed groundbreaking concepts like the "storytelling organization" and "Tamara-land." These ideas gained recognition, shaping my academic reputation. Each bet required foresight, perseverance, and a willingness to embrace uncertainty.

Perspective Sensemaking: Seeing the Future as It Arrives

Making entrepreneurial bets involves what I call "perspective sensemaking." Unlike retrospective sensemaking, which looks backward to draw lessons, perspective sensemaking focuses on envisioning the future as it arrives. This approach aligns with Martin Heidegger's notion of foresight, where past, present, and future are interconnected rather than distinct.

Entrepreneurs engage in perspective sensemaking by crafting narratives that anticipate future opportunities and challenges. These narratives act as guiding plots, helping entrepreneurs align their actions with their vision and adapt to evolving circumstances.

Crafting Purposeful Narratives

To align your plot with bets on the future, you need a narrative that is clear, purposeful, and flexible enough to navigate uncertainty. Here's how to do it:

1. **Start with Your Vision**
   Define the future you're aiming for. What change do you want to create? Your vision is the cornerstone of your narrative and should inspire both you and your stakeholders.
2. **Identify Opportunities and Risks**
   Assess the landscape of your industry or market. What opportunities align with your vision? What risks could derail your plans? Use these insights to craft a narrative that addresses both.

3. **Anticipate Change**
   Build your narrative with the understanding that the future is dynamic. Prepare for multiple scenarios and adapt your story as new information emerges.
4. **Incorporate Emotional Resonance**
   Stories that resonate emotionally are more likely to inspire action. Share personal experiences, challenges, and triumphs to connect with your audience on a deeper level.
5. **Test and Refine Your Narrative**
   Share your story with trusted peers, mentors, or stakeholders. Gather feedback and refine your plot to ensure it aligns with your goals and audience expectations.

Lessons from My Journey

When I look back on my entrepreneurial and academic career, the bets I've made on the future reflect the principles of perspective sensemaking. My father's resilience and ingenuity taught me the value of persistence. My academic achievements, built on storytelling innovations, highlight the importance of aligning your narrative with your vision.

One of the most significant lessons I've learned is that success is not linear. Bets on the future involve risk, and failures are inevitable. What matters is how you adapt, learn, and integrate those lessons into your next story.

Conclusion: The Power of Entrepreneurial Bets

Aligning the plot with bets on the future is both an art and a science. It requires clarity of vision, an understanding of risks and opportunities, and the ability to craft narratives that inspire and guide action. As entrepreneurs, we are not just storytellers—we are sensemakers, shaping the future through the stories we tell.

Whether you're launching a new venture, navigating challenges, or exploring uncharted opportunities, remember this: every bet on the future is a leap of faith. But with purposeful narratives, emotional resonance, and perspective sensemaking, you can turn those leaps into lasting success. Let your story guide you, and the future will follow.

Alvida and David explore the calculated risks in making Bets in the future.

Movie Script and Practical Advice for Entrepreneurs: Aligning the Plot with Bets on the Future

Scene: A Vibrant Training Room in Copenhagen

The room buzzes with energy. Warm light reflects off a sleek wooden table where *David Boje*, *Alvida*, and *Sophie* are seated. Lars, a renowned Danish theater director, strides in confidently, clapping his hands to grab everyone's attention.

Lars: (smiling) *"Today, we'll explore how entrepreneurs can take calculated risks and align their narratives with opportunities and challenges. Ready to dive in?"*

The group nods, intrigued.

Act 1: The Cultural Foundations of Risk

Alvida leans forward, dressed in her signature modern-chic style. Her expression is a mix of excitement and purpose.

Alvida: *"In Denmark, we have a saying: 'Den, der intet vover, intet vinder.' It means, 'Nothing ventured, nothing gained.' Calculated risk-taking is at the heart of our entrepreneurial approach."*

David adjusts his yellow tie and leans back, nodding.

David: *"That aligns with the American entrepreneurial spirit. As Peter Drucker said, 'The best way to predict the future is to create it.' Both philosophies emphasize action, but the strategies differ. Let's explore those differences."*

Lars gestures toward Sophie.

Lars: *"Sophie, you're a Danish entrepreneur navigating your ness growth. Today, you'll learn by observing and participating in role-playing exercises. Let's get started."*

Act 2: A Tale of Two Entrepreneurs

Lars assigns roles to David and Alvida, each embodying distinct entrepreneurial styles.

Lars: *"Alvida, you're launching a sustainable fashion line in Denmark. David, you're an American tech startup founder. Sophie, take notes on their risk strategies."*

Alvida takes a poised stance, channeling her Danish entrepreneurial spirit.

Alvida: (in character) *"We're focused on slow, steady growth. Denmark's social welfare system acts as a safety net, letting us take measured risks with confidence."*

David counters with the bold energy of a Silicon Valley startup founder.

David: (in character) *"In the U.S., we often adopt a high-risk, high-reward approach. I'm pursuing venture capital to scale rapidly. It's risky, but the potential payoff is massive."*

Sophie scribbles notes furiously, captivated by the contrast.

Sophie: *"You both approach risk differently, but the goal seems to be the same: growth through strategic decision-making."*

Act 3: Calculating Risks in Practice

Lars steps in, encouraging a discussion about risk assessment.

Lars: *"Let's talk about the mechanics of calculated risks. How do you decide which risks are worth taking?"*

David steps out of character, speaking directly to Sophie.

David: *"Think of it as a risk-reward ratio. For instance, if a new machine costs $100 but generates $500 in revenue, that's a 5:1 ratio. High return, low relative risk—it's a good bet."*

Alvida adds her perspective, blending cultural insights with business acumen.

Alvida: *"In Denmark, we also consider social impact. If a decision benefits both the business and society, it's easier to justify taking the risk. Our welfare system allows us to innovate without fear of complete financial ruin."*

Act 4: Expanding Horizons

The group transitions to a scenario of market expansion.

Lars: *"This time, focus on how you'd approach growing your businesses into new markets."*

Alvida adjusts her tone, embodying cautious optimism.

Alvida: (in character) *"I'd start by expanding to nearby European markets. Cultural proximity and ease of trade make it a calculated risk."*

David brings a more aggressive approach to the table.

David: (in character) *"I'd go for global expansion. Yes, it's riskier, but the potential rewards are exponentially higher."*

Sophie interjects thoughtfully.

Sophie: *"It seems like Danish entrepreneurs value stability, while Americans prioritize scale and speed."*

Lars smiles, clearly impressed.

Lars: *"Excellent observation, Sophie. Let's apply these lessons to your own business."*

Act 5: Sophie's Takeaways

The group shifts focus to Sophie's entrepreneurial journey.

Lars: *"Sophie, what risks are you facing, and how can you apply what you've learned today?"*

Sophie reflects, inspired by the session.

Sophie: *"I've been hesitant to expand, but now I see how combining Danish caution with American boldness can work. I'll start with nearby markets, but I'll also develop a plan for bigger, riskier opportunities in the future."*

David offers practical advice.

David: *"Remember, entrepreneurship is a game of calculated risk. It's not about blind leaps of faith but informed decisions that push you forward."*

Alvida nods, adding a final thought.

Alvida: *"And don't forget, our welfare systems and networks are tools for innovation, not excuses for complacency. Use them wisely."*

Final Scene: Closing Reflections

Lars gathers the group for a final word.

Lars: *"In entrepreneurship, as in theater, the best performances come from those willing to take risks—but always with preparation and awareness. Balance creativity with practicality, and you'll achieve great things."*

Sophie leaves the room energized and equipped with strategies to take calculated risks while staying aligned with her goals.

Practical Takeaways for Entrepreneurs

1. **Weigh Risks and Rewards:** Use a risk-reward ratio to assess decisions. For example, a 5:1 ratio (spending $100 to gain $500) indicates a worthwhile investment.
2. **Leverage Cultural Strengths:** Danish entrepreneurs benefit from social safety nets, enabling steady, low-risk growth. American entrepreneurs often rely on bold moves and venture capital for rapid scaling. Learn from both approaches.
3. **Expand Strategically:** Start with markets where cultural and trade barriers are minimal before pursuing riskier, high-reward opportunities.

4. **Balance Boldness with Caution:** Combine measured strategies with visionary goals to navigate uncertainty effectively.
5. **Always Prepare:** Risk-taking without preparation leads to failure. Conduct thorough research, build contingency plans, and align your narrative with your vision.

Sophie's journey exemplified how calculated risks and aligned narratives can drive entrepreneurial success. By blending the best of Danish caution and American boldness, she charts a unique, purposeful path forward. Entrepreneurs take note: the future is yours to create. Make your bets wisely.

Chapter 4: "Living Stories with Timing by actively Shaping their spacetimemattering"

Connect Timing and Being: Deliver stories at the right moment while actively shaping their creation.

Alvida and David examine the Being process, exploring how their identity and sense of self inform their entrepreneurial journey.

[The scene continues with Alvida and David sitting outside a cozy outdoor café in Copenhagen, sipping their hot chocolate and engaging in a spirited conversation. It's winter, but they have blankets.]

Alvida: "I've been thinking a lot about my identity as an entrepreneur. Learning the essence of who we are. I used to be an actress, but now am I supposed to be all about business and profit?"

David: "Doesn't have to be like that. I think our sense of self is deeply tied to our entrepreneurial journey to help the world of Being. How do you think your identity has influenced your path toward social entrepreneur life?"

Alvida: "I think it's given me a unique perspective. I'm used to being in the spotlight, taking risks, and adapting to new situations. But as an entrepreneur, I've had to learn to balance my creative impulses for a better world with the practicalities of running a business."

David: "That's a great point. Our sense of self can be both a strength and a weakness in entrepreneurship. But I think Heidegger's concept of Being in the world is relevant here. He argues that our sense of self is not fixed, but rather it emerges from our interactions with the world around us."

Alvida: "I'm not really into Heidegger. Prefer **Soren Kierkegaard's notions of Being and existentialism. He argues that our sense of self is not fixed, but rather it emerges from our experiences and choices** my sense of self is not just about who I am as a person, but also about how I relate to the world around me."

David: "Exactly. And I think that's what makes storytelling so important in entrepreneurship. It's not just about sharing our stories, but it's about creating a sense of connection and bringing something more natural and embodied into the world."

Alvida: "I couldn't agree more. And I think that's what makes this conversation so important. It's not just about our identities and sense of self, but it's about how we relate to animals, plants, rivers, the whole world around us and how we can create real instead of fake sustainability."

David: "Exactly. And I think that's what makes Myra J. Hird's work on the intersections of science, technology, and feminist theory so relevant. She also argues that the distinction between 'second wave' and 'third wave' feminism is problematic, as it implies a linear progression from one wave to the next, rather than acknowledging the complexities and contradictions within and between different feminist movements."

Alvida: "I disagree. And stop with the lecturing. It's kind of condescending. Besides, I think there's a clear distinction between second-wave and third-wave feminism. Second-wave feminism was all about equality and sameness, while third-wave feminism is about diversity and intersectionality."

David: "Forgive the lecture. It is what I have experienced? People do think that second-wave feminism was just a precursor to third-wave feminism, but do you admit that we're still grappling with the same issues of inequality and oppression?"

Alvida: "Let's agree to disagree. I think second-wave feminism was a necessary step toward equality, but it was limited in its scope and didn't address the complexities of intersectionality. Third-wave feminism is a more nuanced and inclusive movement that recognizes the diversity of women's experiences."

David: "OK, as an alternative, consider Karen Barad. She talks about how our sense of self is not separate from the world around us, but rather it's an integral part of it. Barad argues that the distinction between "second wave" and "third wave" feminism is problematic, as it implies a linear progression from one wave to the next..."

Alvida: "No, I don't think so. And are you seriously instructing me about Barad? I think recognizing our differences is essential to creating a more just and equitable society. And I think that's what makes entrepreneurship so exciting - it's not just about making a profit or achieving success, but it's about creating a positive impact on the world around us. Oh, this is so frustrating."

(Just as the argument is escalating, a strange, glowing light fills the room. Alvida and David look around, confused, as the light grows brighter and begins to take shape.)

Alvida: "What's going on?"

David: "I have no idea, but I think we're in trouble."

(The light coalesces into a figure, a tall, statuesque woman with long, flowing hair and a kind face. She introduces herself as Hilda, a Danish Shaman.)

Hilda: "Greetings, travelers. I sense that you are both carrying heavy burdens. I have come to take you on a journey to help you find balance and harmony."

Alvida: "What kind of journey?"

Hilda: "A journey to the Inn of the Arts in Las Cruces, New Mexico. It is a place of great beauty and creativity, where you will find the answers, you seek."

(With a wave of her hand, Hilda transports Alvida and David to the Inn of the Arts, a charming bed and breakfast nestled in the heart of Las Cruces.)

Alvida: "Where are we?"

David: "I have no idea, but I think we're in New Mexico."

Hilda: "You are true. And you will find that this place has much to teach you about the power of art and creativity to bring people together and heal the world."

(As they explore the inn, Alvida and David begin to see the world in a new light, and their differences begin to fade away. They discover that they have more in common than they thought and that their shared humanity is stronger than any disagreement.)

Alvida starts: "I think Donna Haraway's idea of staying with the trouble is also relevant here. She argues that we need to stay with the trouble and uncertainty of the world, rather than trying to control or dominate it."

David: "Haraway's work on cyborgs and the "informatics of domination" can be seen as a critique of the notion of a singular, coherent "second wave" or "third wave" feminism, instead highlighting how these movements are shaped by and respond to the complexities of technology, capitalism, and globalization.

(As they explore the inn, Alveda and David begin to see the world in a new light, and their differences begin to fade away. They discover that they have more in common than they thought and that their shared humanity is stronger than any disagreement.)

"Precisely," David responds. "It's like Donna Haraway's idea of 'staying with the trouble.' We're not separate from the world, but part of its ongoing story."

Alvida noted, "This reminds me of something Yvon Chouinard, founder of Patagonia, once said: 'The more you know, the less you need.' It's about recognizing the agency in all things."

David: "I never thought I'd say this, but I think I'm starting to understand you, Alvida."

Alvida: "And I think I'm starting to understand you, David. We're not so different after all."

Hilda: "Ah, I knew you two would find common ground. And now, I must take my leave. But remember, the power of art and creativity is always available to you, whenever you need it."

(With a final smile, Hilda seems to fade, leaving Alvida and David to continue their journey of discovery and growth.)

[The scene fades to black as Alvida and David continue their conversation, exploring the complexities of identity, sense of self, and entrepreneurship. Hilda just disappears into the light]

Practical Quotes from entrepreneurs from Denmark and Sweden:
1. "As an entrepreneur, I've learned to be comfortable with uncertainty and to adapt to new situations." - Trine Søndergaard, Danish entrepreneur
2. "My sense of self is deeply tied to my entrepreneurial journey. I've always been driven by a desire to create something new and innovative." - Anders Holch Povlsen, Danish entrepreneur.
3. It's like what Maersk Mc-Kinney Møller once said: 'The most important thing is to have a goal, and then have the courage to follow it.'
4. "I think my identity as a Swede has influenced my entrepreneurial path. I've always been proud of my Swedish heritage and have tried

to incorporate that into my business." - Sofia Åkerman, Swedish entrepreneur.
5. "As an entrepreneur, I've learned to be resilient and to take calculated risks. It's not always easy, but it's worth it in the end." - Lars Kolind, Danish entrepreneur.
6. "I think my sense of self is constantly evolving as an entrepreneur. I'm always learning and growing, and that's what makes it so exciting." - Anna-Karin Hatt, Swedish entrepreneur.

Practical Quotes Entrepreneurs from Canada and USA:
1. "As an entrepreneur, I've learned to be comfortable with uncertainty and to adapt to new situations. It's not always easy, but it's worth it in the end." - Arlene Dickinson, Canadian entrepreneur.
2. "My sense of self is deeply tied to my entrepreneurial journey. I've always been driven by a desire to create something new and innovative." - Sara Blakely, American entrepreneur.
3. "I think my identity as a Canadian has influenced my entrepreneurial path. I've always been proud of my Canadian heritage and have tried to incorporate that into my business." - Michael Wekerle, Canadian entrepreneur.
4. "As an entrepreneur, I've learned to be resilient and to take calculated risks. It's not always easy, but it's worth it in the end." - Richard Branson, American entrepreneur.
5. "I think my sense of self is constantly evolving as an entrepreneur. I'm always learning and growing, and that's what makes it so exciting." - Lisa Nichols, American entrepreneur.
6. 'The only way to do great work is to love what you do" Steve Jobs, an American entrepreneur.

How to Connect the Timing principle of 'True Storytelling®' and 'Being' process of Boje's Antenarrative to Entrepreneurship?

Read On if you want more depth into Timing & Being.

True Storytelling Principle 4: "**Timing:** You must have timing."
Antenarrative Process 4: "Being: Our identity and sense of self is our entrepreneurial journey."

Short Answer: "Deliver Stories at the Right Moment While Actively Shaping Their Creation"

Introduction: Aligning Timing with Being

Timing is critical in True Storytelling® (Larsen, Boje, & Bruun, 2020), whether in entrepreneurial ventures, organizational change, or individual narratives. David Boje and Rohny Saylor's (2023) concept of *Being* in antenarrative pre-storying emphasizes shaping narratives in the flow of time, both prospectively and retrospectively. This chapter explores how Boje's antenarrative concepts align with Martin Heidegger's (1927) *Being and Time*, Karen Barad's (2007, 2010, 2017) *spacetimemattering*, Karl Weick's (1995) sensemaking, and Lou Pondy's *enthinkment* (https://enthinkment.com). Together, these theories provide a rich framework for understanding how timing shapes the antenarratives we live by, our enthinking, and the futures we create.

Martin Heidegger: The Horizon of Being and Timing

Heidegger's *Being and Time* (1927) investigates the temporality of existence, questioning how Being unfolds within and beyond time. For Heidegger, conventional notions of time—clock time, calendar time, or singular moments—are insufficient to grasp the essence of Being. He proposes that temporality is *primordial*, not limited to human sensemaking or linear histories. Heidegger's concept of *care* underpins the idea that humans are always projecting themselves toward the future, anticipating possibilities while carrying the weight of their past.

Boje extends Heidegger's temporality by incorporating *antenarrative* processes that acknowledge both *prospective sensemaking*—the act of betting on futures—and the continual restorying of unsettled pasts through *Before* narratives. Boje's antenarrative acts as a bridge between Heidegger's *primordial time* and storytelling, emphasizing that the timing of a story is as vital as its content. Delivering a story at the right moment, as Boje suggests, requires an acute awareness of the *temporal horizon* Heidegger describes—one that integrates past, present, and future into a unified unfolding.

Karen Barad: Spacetimemattering and Boje Storytelling

While Heidegger situates temporality in human experience, Karen Barad's concept of *spacetimemattering* challenges anthropocentric views of time. Barad (2010) argues that time, space, and matter are inseparable, entangled in what she calls *intra-activity*. For Barad, moments are not discrete; they are diffractive, threaded through one another in complex relationships that defy linearity.

Boje aligns with Barad's framework by emphasizing that storytelling is not merely a human act but an intra-active process. Stories emerge in the Becoming process of antenarrative (Jørgensen & Boje, 2009) within the entanglements of materiality and discourse. For example, a company's decision to launch a new product is shaped not only by its leaders' narratives but also by market dynamics, technological constraints, and societal trends—all of which are inseparably woven into *spacetimemattering*. Boje's concept of timing in storytelling resonates with Barad's view that moments are holographic and relational, requiring storytellers to remain attuned to the multiple temporalities that shape their narratives.

Louis Pondy and Karl Weick: Enthinkment and Enactment

Louis Pondy's notion of *enthinkment*, as interpreted by Boje and Saylors (2023), adds another dimension to the discussion. *Enthinkment* suggests that ideas and narratives emerge through reflective thought, an ongoing dialogue between past experiences and future possibilities. Unlike Karl Weick's retrospective sensemaking, which focuses on making sense of past events, *enthinkment* allows for *prospective sensemaking*, aligning closely with Boje's antenarrative approach.

Weick's sensemaking, grounded in enactment and the five human senses, emphasizes the active role of individuals in constructing meaning. Boje builds on this by arguing that sensemaking is not limited to the retrospective. His concept of *Bets on the Future* suggests that individuals and organizations actively shape their trajectories by imagining and enacting multiple potential futures. Timing, in this context, involves recognizing the right moment to act—a blend of *enthinkment* and Weick's enactment, enriched by antenarrative foresight.

Boje's Antenarrative: Being and Timing in Storytelling
Boje's antenarrative processes—particularly *Being* and *Before*—bridge these philosophical and theoretical perspectives, offering practical insights for storytelling. The *Being* process focuses on the present moment, emphasizing the act of creation as stories unfold. This aligns with Heidegger's *Being-in-the-world*, where existence is rooted in care and attunement to temporality. However, Boje extends Heidegger's framework by introducing the *Before* antenarrative, which highlights the multiplicity of pasts that inform and shape the present.

In practice, Boje's antenarrative helps entrepreneurs and organizations connect timing with storytelling by:
8. **Recognizing Temporal Entanglements:** Stories are not isolated; they are part of larger temporal networks that include cultural histories, organizational contexts, and material realities.
9. **Betting on Futures:** Antenarrative encourages storytellers to anticipate and shape emerging opportunities while remaining grounded in the lessons of the past.
10. **Adapting to Context:** Delivering a story at the right moment requires sensitivity to the temporal and material conditions in which it is told.

Practical Application: Timing in True Storytelling

To connect timing with *Being* in storytelling, practitioners can use the following strategies:

10. **Synchronize with Context:** Analyze the temporal and material dynamics of your audience. For example, launching a marketing campaign requires aligning the narrative with market trends, societal sentiments, and technological readiness.
11. **Leverage Antenarrative Processes:** Use *Before* antenarratives to uncover untold histories that resonate with your audience, and *Bets on the Future* to craft forward-looking narratives that inspire action.
12. **Embrace Intra-activity:** Recognize that stories are co-created within entangled systems of people, technology, and materiality. Timing requires an awareness of these entanglements.
13. **Incorporate Multiple Temporalities:** Like Barad's diffractive time, storytelling should acknowledge overlapping pasts, presents, and futures. This approach ensures that narratives are multidimensional and adaptive.
14. **Practice Enthinkment:** Reflect on the interplay of past experiences and future possibilities to create stories that are both grounded and visionary.

Conclusion: Storytelling Beyond Linear Time

By connecting timing with *Being*, Boje's antenarrative integrates Heidegger's philosophical depth, Barad's quantum relationality, Pondy's reflective *enthinkment*, and Weick's enactment. This alignment offers a comprehensive framework for delivering stories at the right moment while actively shaping their creation.

Storytelling, in Boje's view, is not just a retrospective act of making sense of what has already occurred. It is a dynamic process that involves betting on the future, entangling multiple temporalities, and embracing the material-discursive interplay of *spacetimemattering*. Practitioners who master this approach can create narratives that resonate deeply, adapt to changing contexts, and inspire transformative action. By aligning timing with *Being*, storytellers can transcend the constraints of linear time and open new horizons of possibility.

References

Ajvazi, I. (n.d.). *Heidegger: Being and becoming.* Retrieved from https://philarchive.org/archive/AJVHBA#:~:text=Heidegger%20views%20temporality%20as%20the,in%20the%20world%20of%20things

Barad, K. (2010). Quantum entanglements and hauntological relations of inheritance: Dis/continuities, spacetime enfoldings, and justice-to-come. *Derrida Today, 3*(2), 240–268. https://doi.org/10.3366/drt.2010.0206

Barad, K. (2017). Troubling time/s and ecologies of nothingness: Re-turning, re-membering, and facing the incalculable. *New Formations, 92*(92), 56–86. https://doi.org/10.3898/newf:92.04.2017

Boje, D. (2001). Narrative methods for organizational & communication research. Thousand Oaks, CA: Sage.

Boje, D. M. (2012). Reflections: What does quantum physics of storytelling mean for change management? *Journal of Change Management, 12*(3), 253–271. https://doi.org/10.1080/14697017.2012.674648

Boje, D. M. (2014). *Storytelling organizational practices: Managing in the quantum age.* Routledge.

Boje, D. M. (2018). Quantum storytelling consulting, ensemble leadership theory, and world ecology. In *The Emerald Handbook of Quantum Storytelling Consulting* (pp. 21–33). Emerald Publishing Limited. https://doi.org/10.1108/978-1-78743-404-820181003

Boje, David (2024). "The Entrepreneur's Storytelling Journey: Danish and American Guide to Crafting Compelling Entrepreneur-Storytelling using the Seven Antenarrative Processes (Quantum Storytelling)" https://www.amazon.com/Entrepreneurs-Storytelling-Journey-Entrepreneur-Storytelling-Antenarrative/dp/B0DQNNSCRT

Boje, D. M., & Saylors, R. (2023). *The management thought of Louis R. Pondy: Reclaiming the enthinkment path.* Taylor & Francis.

Heidegger, M. (1927). *Being and time.* (J. Macquarrie & E. Robinson, Trans.). Harper & Row. (Original work published in German).

Jørgensen, K. M., & Boje, D. M. (2009). GENEALOGIES OF BECOMING-ANTENARRATIVE INQUIRY IN ORGANIZATIONS. *Tamara Journal for Critical Organization Inquiry, 8.* **Vol 8 Issue 8.1 September: pp. 32-47 ISSN 1532-5555** Online.

Larsen, J., Boje, D. M., & Bruun, L. (2020). *True storytelling: Seven principles for an ethical and sustainable change-management strategy.* Routledge.

Weick, K. E. (1995). *Sensemaking in organizations.* Sage Publications.

Chapter 5: "Helping Stories Along by Restorying Your Little Wow Moments into a New Story"

Antenarrative Process 4: **Becoming**: The transformation and growth we experience as entrepreneurs.

True Storytelling® Principle 4: **Help stories along: You must be able to help stories on their way and be open to experiment.**

Answer: To Pair Help Stories Along with Becoming: Nurture evolving narratives by staying open to experimentation and transformation.

Becoming a Successful Entrepreneur: Restorying Your Journey

Setting: A rustic yet modern cabin surrounded by Danish countryside. A crackling fire warms the room as Hilda, the shaman and storytelling coach, prepares tea for her guests. Alvida, David, and Sophie sit at a wooden table covered with notebooks, markers, and blank pages for brainstorming.

Hilda: (smiling warmly) Welcome, Sophie. Alvida and David have told me a lot about your entrepreneurial spirit. Today, we'll explore how storytelling can not only shape your journey but transform it.

Sophie: (excited) Thank you. I'm here to learn how to make my entrepreneurial story more impactful. I want to connect with my audience and bring my vision to life.

David: That's a fantastic goal, Sophie. Storytelling is about more than just words. It's about *being*—aligning your story with your values and actions.

Alvida: And it's also about *becoming*. Stories evolve just as we do. That's where restorying comes in—reframing your narrative to align with who you're becoming.

The Restorying Steps

Hilda: (placing a tea tray on the table) Let's begin with the first step: *Characterize*. Sophie, tell us about your business at its best. If it were functioning perfectly, what would it look like?

Sophie: (pausing thoughtfully) It would be a community-centered brand that empowers people through sustainable practices. I want my business to inspire trust and collaboration.

Hilda: Wonderful. Now, we create an influence map. (She draws a large circle on paper.) Who influences your business, and who or what does your business influence?

Sophie identifies key players: her customers, collaborators, and the environment, mapping their interconnected relationships.

David: This step helps us understand the *state of affairs*—where things are now and where they could be in the future.

Hilda: Next is *Externalize*. Let's treat your main challenge as a character in your story. What's the biggest problem your business faces?

Sophie: (hesitant) I'd say it's "doubt"—both my own and my customer'.

Alvida: Let's call it "The Doubter." Imagine The Doubter as a separate character. How does it behave?

Sophie: (smiling) It whispers questions like, "Can I succeed? Will people trust me?"

David: Great work! By externalizing, you distance yourself from the problem. Now, The Doubter is just one character in your story—not *you*.

Hilda: Step three is *Sympathto ize*. What benefits does The Doubter bring?

Sophie: (surprised) Benefits? Hmm... I suppose it keeps me grounded. It pushes me to double-check my decisions and improve my business.

Alvida: Exactly. Every challenge has a purpose. But now, let's explore step four: *Revise*. What are the negative consequences of letting The Doubter control your story?

Sophie: It holds me back. I spend too much time second-guessing and miss opportunities.

David: That's where commitment to change comes in. Revising the narrative gives you the power to reframe those consequences.

Hilda: (nodding) Step five is to *Strategize*. Think of a time when The Doubter wasn't in control—a moment when you overcame fear and succeeded.

Sophie: Last year, I pitched my idea to a group of investors. I was terrified, but I trusted my story and secured funding.

Alvida: That's a *Little Wow Moment*! It's proof that you can overcome challenges.

David: Now for step six: *Rehistoricize*. Let's take that success and make it the new norm in your story.

Sophie: (writing) So instead of saying, "I doubt myself," I can say, "I'm someone who faces challenges and succeeds."

Hilda: Beautiful. And the final step is to p*ublicize*. Who can support this new narrative?

Sophie: My mentors, my team, and my customers.

Alvida: (smiling) Perfect. Share this story with them. Let them see the confident, resilient entrepreneur you're becoming.

Reflecting on the Journey

Hilda: (leaning back) Sophie, you've done remarkable work today. How do you feel?

Sophie: (beaming) Empowered. I see my story in a completely new light.

David: That's the power of restorying. It transforms not just how others see you, but how you see yourself.

Alvida: And remember, Sophie, storytelling is an ongoing process. Your narrative will keep evolving as you grow.

Hilda: (raising her tea) To Sophie's journey and the stories yet to come. May they be bold, authentic, and transformative.

The group clinks their mugs in a toast as the scene fades, leaving Sophie with renewed confidence and a clear path forward.

Key Takeaways for Entrepreneurs

1. **Reframe Challenges**: Treat obstacles as characters in your story that can be managed or rewritten.
2. **Celebrate Wins**: Focus on Little Wow Moments to inspire confidence and growth.
3. **Engage Your Network**: Share your new narrative with supporters to build momentum.
4. **Be Open to Change**: Embrace restorying as a continuous process of becoming.
5. **Stay Authentic**: Let your values and vision guide your entrepreneurial journey.

As Sophie discovered, the key to entrepreneurial success lies in embracing transformation, crafting meaningful stories, and trusting the journey. What story will you tell?

Practical Tips for Entrepreneurs' Storytelling:
1. Be authentic and vulnerable: Share your struggles and successes and be willing to learn from your mistakes.
2. Connect with your audience: Use storytelling to build trust and rapport with your audience, and to convey your message in a way that resonates.
3. Use indigenous practices: Incorporate traditional storytelling techniques into your marketing strategies and use ancient wisdom to navigate the challenges of modern business.

4. Share your personal story: Use your personal story to connect with your audience, and to convey your values and mission.
5. Practice mindfulness: Take time to reflect on your journey, and to tap into the wisdom of the universe.

Entrepreneurship plays an important role in Scandinavian economies. In Sweden, many people start businesses for non-economic reasons, such as a desire for independence[9]. Indigenous entrepreneurship is also present in northern Sweden, particularly among the Sami people. Sami businesses often incorporate traditional knowledge and cultural practices, balancing market participation with cultural preservation[5].

Some key sectors for Sami entrepreneurs include reindeer husbandry, handicrafts, tourism, and food processing. However, Sami businesses face unique challenges related to land use conflicts and regulatory barriers.

Practical Tips for Entrepreneurs' Storytelling:
1. Be authentic and vulnerable: Share your struggles and successes and be willing to learn from your mistakes.
2. Connect with your audience: Use storytelling to build trust and rapport with your audience, and to convey your message in a way that resonates.
3. Use indigenous practices: Incorporate traditional storytelling techniques into your marketing strategies and use ancient wisdom to navigate the challenges of modern business.
4. Share your personal story: Use your personal story to connect with your audience, and to convey your values and mission.
5. Practice mindfulness: Take time to reflect on your journey, and to tap into the wisdom of the universe.
6. Use storytelling to build community: Use storytelling to connect with others, and to build a sense of community and belonging.

7. Be patient and persistent: Building a successful business takes time and effort, so be patient and persistent in your storytelling efforts.

To support Indigenous entrepreneurship, recommendations include:
Improving data collection on Indigenous livelihoods
1. Making development programs more inclusive
2. Addressing regulatory and financial barriers
3. Enhancing Indigenous rights and governance

For entrepreneurs in general, storytelling can be an effective tool for communicating vision and values. Practical tips for entrepreneurial storytelling might include:
1. Authentically sharing your journey and motivations
2. Highlighting how you've overcome challenges
3. Connecting your story to your target audience
4. Using narrative techniques like vivid details and emotion

We hope these insights about entrepreneurship in Scandinavia and storytelling tips are helpful. Let me know if you need any clarification or have other questions I can assist with.

Success as an entrepreneur isn't just about profits and products—it's about transformation. David Boje's *Entrepreneur's Storytelling Journey* introduces a practical framework for navigating this transformation using three key antenarrative processes:
1. **Restory the Before** – Revisit and reinterpret past experiences.
2. **Reimagine Your Identity in Being** – Understand and reshape who you are as an entrepreneur.
3. **Make a New Bet on the Future** – Craft forward-looking strategies that align with your goals.

The cornerstone of this journey is a process called **restorying**: rewriting the narrative of your entrepreneurial life by drawing lessons from the past, finding clarity in the present, and betting on future opportunities.

Restorying for Entrepreneurs: The Big Picture

Entrepreneurship is a dynamic process that involves more than just managing your business—it's about aligning your story with your values, goals, and vision. Restorying involves uncovering what Boje calls *Little Wow Moments*: pivotal experiences that reveal untapped potential. By reframing these moments, you can build a new narrative that inspires growth, resilience, and purpose.

Boje emphasizes that storytelling is no longer about a singular voice dictating the past; it's about collaboration and diversity. For entrepreneurs, this means negotiating how the story of your business integrates the past, present, and future to resonate with your audience and stakeholders.

Seven Practical Steps for Entrepreneurial Restorying

Step 1: Characterize Your True Identity Start by imagining your business (or yourself) at its best. What would success look like if your organization were living up to its ideals?

15. **Exercise**: Create an "influence map" to explore how key individuals and problems interact.

What is the current state of your business?
How do problems impact relationships and operations?
What future can you envision based on these insights?

Step 2: Externalize the Problem Reframe challenges as separate from yourself or your business. This shift allows you to view problems as manageable, external factors rather than insurmountable personal failures.

- **Example**: Instead of saying, "I can't manage my time," reframe it as "Time management is a challenge I can improve."

Step 3: Sympathize with the Problem Identify how the problem might be benefiting your business or habits. This step reveals hidden dynamics that perpetuate the issue.
- **Exercise**: Explore both sides of the problem. What beliefs or practices support it? What are the pros and cons of these dynamics?

Step 4: Revise for Commitment to Change Examine the downsides of the problem. Would you truly benefit from overcoming it?
- **Example**: Acknowledge how being overworked may harm creativity or relationships, strengthening your resolve to implement change.

Step 5: Strategize with Unique Outcomes Find moments when the problem was less impactful or when you succeeded despite challenges. These are your *Little Wow Moments*.
- **Exercise**: Identify times when you resisted the problem. What behaviors, choices, or circumstances contributed to those successes?

Step 6: Rehistoricize the Narrative Turn exceptions into the rule. Build a new story where success and positive change are the norm.
- **Example**: Instead of viewing a past triumph as a fluke, position it as evidence of your potential to consistently overcome obstacles.

Step 7: Publicize and Build a Support Network Share your new narrative with people who can champion your transformation. Their support reinforces your progress and keeps you accountable.
1. **Exercise**: Identify mentors, colleagues, or community members who can help you maintain this new direction.

Practical Example: From Problem to Potential
Case Study: Time Management for Growth
Before Restorying: An entrepreneur struggles with time management, leading to missed opportunities and burnout. The problem feels personal and overwhelming.
Applying the Steps:
1. **Characterize**: Envision running a business where priorities are clear, and time is optimized.

2. **Externalize**: Treat poor time management as a separate entity—a "gremlin" that can be managed.
3. **Sympathize**: Recognize how the problem might provide a sense of control (e.g., handling everything yourself) while acknowledging its limitations.
4. **Revise**: Acknowledge how the "gremlin" hinders growth and creativity.
5. **Strategize**: Recall a day when clear delegation allowed you to focus on high-impact tasks.
6. **Rehistoricize**: Frame delegation as a key factor in achieving long-term goals.
7. **Publicize**: Share your new approach with your team, creating a culture of accountability and collaboration.

Result: The entrepreneur adopts structured time management practices and builds a team culture that supports growth.

Betting on the Future: Aligning with Your Vision

One of the most powerful aspects of restorying is making **Bets on the Future**. This means using the insights from your past and present to shape actionable, forward-thinking strategies. Successful entrepreneurs don't just react to change—they actively anticipate and influence it.
- **Forecast Opportunities**: Identify trends and shifts in your industry.
- **Anticipate Challenges**: Use past experiences to foresee and address potential roadblocks.
- **Build Resilience**: Create a narrative that inspires adaptability and innovation.

Restorying for Entrepreneurs: Practical Tips
- **Revisit Your Why**: Constantly align your actions with your core values and purpose.
- **Embrace Little Wow Moments**: Celebrate small wins and use them as building blocks for larger transformations.
- **Be Open to Collaboration**: Engage with diverse voices and perspectives to enrich your narrative.

- **Invest in Reflection**: Dedicate time to evaluate past experiences and identify patterns that influence your decisions.
- **Stay Flexible**: Adapt your story as circumstances evolve, keeping your vision at the forefront.

Conclusion: Transform Your Story, Transform Your Business

Restorying is more than a narrative tool; it's a transformative process that empowers entrepreneurs to reimagine their identities, overcome challenges, and create meaningful futures. By integrating the past, present, and future into a cohesive story, you can unlock new opportunities and achieve sustainable success.

Your entrepreneurial journey is a story in progress. Embrace the power of restorying to shape that story—and your future—on your terms.

References

Boje, D. M. (2013, December). Quantum restorying of the PTSD Leviathan: Posthumanist, critical new materialisms of wider agentic-trauma of military and civilian bodies. In *Proceedings of the 3rd Annual Quantum Storytelling Conference, Las Cruces, NM*. https://davidboje.com/vita/paper_pdfs/Posthumanist%20Quantum%20Restorying%20PROCEEDING%20Boje%202013.pdf

Boje, D. M. (2014). *Storytelling organizational practices: Managing in the quantum age*. Routledge.

Boje, D.M. & Rosile, G.A. (2015, March). *Equine-assisted restorying for veterans and their loved ones*. Presentation at the annual conference of the Equine Assisted Growth and Learning Association (EAGALA), Utah.

Flora, J., Boje, D., Rosile, G. A., & Hacker, K. (2016). A theoretical and applied review of embodied restorying for post-deployment family reintegration. *Journal of Veterans Studies*, *1*(1), 129-162. https://pdfs.semanticscholar.org/cf83/1c88ec40a66c552ca2159044477f95c063aa.pdf

Rosile, G. A. (1998b) Restorying and the Case of the Sci-Fi Organization. Academy of Management Presentation. http://web.nmsu.edu/~garosile/garscifiacademy.html

Rosile, G. A., & Boje, D. M. (2002). Restorying and postmodern organization theatre: Consultation in the storytelling organization. *Changing the way we manage change*, 271-290.

Rosile, G. A. and Dennehy, R. H. (1998) Restorying for Personal and Organizational Change. Proceedings of the Southwest Academy of Management, 14th annual meeting in Dallas, Texas, March 5-7, (pp. 275-276).

White, M., & Epston, D. (1990). *Narrative means to therapeutic ends*. New York, NY: Norton & Company.

Chapter 6: "Staging with artifacts and scenes to Communicate to the Four Who's"

Link Staging with Between: Use settings, artifacts, and relationships to create immersive storytelling experiences.

True Storytelling® Principle 6: Staging: You must consider staging including scenography and artifacts.

Antenarrative Process 6 The Between: The connections and relationships we build with others.

Our purpose is to link the Between-the-Who's to the Staging of Scenography and artifacts to create immersive entrepreneurship storytelling experiences for your audience. THE FOUR WHOs is about the audience that your storytelling is supposed to reach in staging your scenography and artifacts:

By this point in the book, you have enough skills and the principles and processes for the entrepreneur's storytelling journey to take this next step. It's about framing your communication to a particular audience and identifying the scenes the artifacts, and what I call the four who's of this audience.

Movie Script: Building Scene and Artifact Connections Between the Who's

Setting: Hilda's cozy cabin, nestled in a forest clearing, surrounded by tall trees and the gentle hum of nature. A crackling fire warms the room as sunlight filters through the wooden shutters.

Characters:
1. **Hilda:** A wise Danish shaman, guiding the group through the concept of the Between.
2. **Alvida:** A Danish entrepreneur seeking deeper connections in her storytelling approach.
3. **David:** An American storytelling expert exploring the role of scenography and artifacts in entrepreneurship.
4. **Sophie:** A young, eager Danish entrepreneur looking for guidance in her journey.

Scene 1: The Cabin Conversation
Hilda places a tray of traditional Danish pastries on the table, the aroma filling the room. Alvida and David sip on herbal tea as Sophie joins them, her eyes filled with curiosity.

Hilda: "The Between is more than a concept—it's a sacred space. It's where we connect, with nature, and with the wisdom that flows through the universe. Entrepreneurs often overlook this, focusing too much on products and profit. But true success begins with relationships."

Alvida: "I've always felt that storytelling is how we bridge those gaps. When we share our experiences authentically, we create trust and understanding. But how do we make those connections more tangible?"

David: "Through scenography and artifacts. Every entrepreneur can craft a story that immerses their audience. The way we stage our story, the objects we use, and the emotions we evoke—these are the threads that weave the Between."

Sophie leans forward, intrigued.

Sophie: "So, how do I start? How do I use these ideas to connect with my audience?"

Scene 2: Hands-On Learning
Hilda retrieves a wooden box filled with small artifacts: marbles, tiny figurines, natural stones, and pieces of colored fabric. She places a shallow sand tray on the table.

Hilda: "Let's practice. This sand tray is your canvas. Choose artifacts to represent the Four Who's in your entrepreneurial story: your ego, your relationships, the institutions you engage with, and the environment you wish to impact."

Sophie hesitates before selecting a few items: a small stone to symbolize resilience, a green leaf for sustainability, and a figurine of a family to represent her relationships.

David: "Now, imagine your audience. Which artifacts resonate with them? Which ones don't? Remove what doesn't connect and add new elements to reflect their values and aspirations."

Sophie replaces the green leaf with a seashell, symbolizing her audience's connection to the ocean.
Alvida: "This is how we stage our stories. Each artifact becomes part of a scene that speaks to the audience's heart. It's not just about showing what we value; it's about inviting them into a shared narrative."

Scene 3: The Forest Walk
The group ventures into the forest, the sunlight dappling through the leaves. Hilda leads them to a clearing with a large rock overlooking a valley. The sound of a gentle stream fills the air.
Hilda: "This is scenography in its purest form. Notice the natural elements around you—the textures, the colors, the sounds. When you craft your story, think of these sensory details. They anchor your audience in the moment."
Sophie: "It's like creating a stage for my story, where every detail matters. But how do I ensure it connects with my audience?"
David: "By understanding the Four Who's. Are you speaking from your ego, focusing on yourself? Or are you addressing the social, corporate, or ecological concerns of your audience? Each story must balance these perspectives."
Alvida: "And don't forget the artifacts. They're not just props—they're symbols. They tell a story within the story."

Scene 4: Reflecting on the Valley
The group sits on the large rock, overlooking the valley. Sophie looks thoughtful as she arranges a few small stones she picked up along the trail.
Sophie: "I see now that the Between isn't just about relationships. It's about how we stage those relationships—through scenes, artifacts, and shared moments."
Hilda: "Exactly. The Between is a sacred space where connections deepen and wisdom flows. When you honor that space, your story becomes more than words—it becomes an experience."

David: "That's why artifacts and scenography are so powerful. They give your story texture, depth, and resonance. They make the audience feel part of the narrative."

Alvida: "And when we build those connections authentically, the impact is lasting. It's not just about telling your story—it's about inviting others to see themselves in it."

Scene 5: Practical Takeaways

Back in the cabin, the group sits around the fire, jotting down notes and reflections.

David: "Let's summarize what we've learned. First, identify the Four Who's: ego, social, corporate, and ecological. Understand how they interact and which ones resonate most with your audience."

Alvida: "Next, use artifacts to stage your story. Each item should symbolize something meaningful—your values, your audience's needs, or the shared narrative you're building."

Hilda: "And finally, consider scenography. Whether it's a physical space, a digital platform, or an event, every detail should reflect the heart of your story."

Sophie nods, her notebook filled with ideas.

Sophie: "This changes everything. I can see how to use these strategies to create deeper connections with my audience. Thank you."

Hilda: "Remember, the Between is always there. It's up to you to honor it and let it guide your storytelling."

Quotes for Entrepreneurs:

1. **Hilda:** "The Between is a sacred space where connections deepen and wisdom flows. Honor it, and your story will resonate."
2. **David:** "Artifacts and scenography give your story texture and depth. They turn words into experiences."
3. **Alvida:** "When you stage your story authentically, you invite your audience to become part of it."

This script illustrates how entrepreneurs can practically apply the principles of scenography and artifacts to their storytelling, emphasizing the importance of understanding the Four WHO's and honoring the sacred space of the Between.

It's time to think about the products or services that you providing to customers. We introduced four hearts in true storytelling.

You've already got training in three of the hearts and the final chapter will deal with the fourth so let's review. First is the beneath heart that we covered in the first chapter. It has to do with your values and passions. The question is what scenes in your storytelling and what artifacts are going to appeal to the beneath heart? The second heart was in the second chapter of this book and it has to do with the before. It's an atonement for the little moments that were used later in the restoring process so we could gather those little wild moments and create a new story. The third heart is the bat's heart, and its atonement to the future. It can be a retrospective since making of your past entrepreneurial experience put together with an atonement by prospective sense, making to the future, that's arriving in your business and for your customers.

What is Between the Four Hearts?

One way to think about this is it's like a force field between the four hearts and you're trying to figure out how to impact that force field with your storytelling. Figure out if your storytelling is gonna be from the ego that your ego is all about you. Second, is the storytelling gonna be about the social who so about your family about your relationships in society your friends, your comrades? Third it could be about what we call the corporate so corporate could be government education, military university, or just a plain old corporation the corporate tends to dominate your own egoistic sometimes you need a good ego Perate, who can dominate the social who and so we park our social concerns at the door, but let's look at the fourth who and it's the ecological who is it particularly important when we're talking about true storytelling because that's all about creating opportunities for sustainability. But the question is is it a greenwashing of sustainability or is it a statement of true storytelling of sustainability? Another way to think about the force field of the four hearts and the going in between those hearts where we find the four is that it's a kind of an energy field of the vibrant mattering energy field. We called in quantum storytelling following the work of Jane Bennett. So we're creating vibes to the hose that are important in our communication as an entrepreneur to particular audiences.

My path in dealing with the beyond heart which will cover the next chapter you know when we're going into the unknown is beyond our five senses of Weick's 1995 enactment.

We do a protreptic exploration of the four hearts and the four who-consciousness. This is so important, your existence in Being. True storytelling (Larsen, Boje, & Bruun, 2021) asks some questions of participants, to get back to 'what's true' in the uncovering of Being. Understanding the hearts and the who's is a way to unfold the process.

So let's review the four whose so I want to give you a little bit of storytelling around each one because this is a brand new theory and thank you for listening.

The Four Who's of Effective Entrepreneur Communication

Ego-Who-Consciousness People and animals have ego-consciousness foregrounded and miss why the Beneath-process is important in life. It's important in life to go underneath (beneath) the iceberg's surface. Going beneath the surface of something, beneath the superficial to something being neglected.

Corporate-Who-Consciousness To go beneath the corporate-who, its bounded rationality consciousness, its foregrounding of people as resources and things as resources, neglects the 'who' of Being-in-the-world. Nature becomes a 'they', and 'Othering' takes place in bounded rationality, so foregrounded in organization studies.

Social-Who-Consciousness The we-consciousness is a reduction in people's relationships, people networking, and communication. The downside of we-consciousness is what Heidegger (1927/1962) calls the 'they-self.' The reduction to human relations, the 'they-self' beckons, and can take over the authentic self.

Ecological-Who-Consciousness The eco-consciousness science becomes the one that observes and interprets the things of nature. Nature sciences have their own privileged and foregrounded consciousness. "… who are encountered along with environmental things" (Heidegger, 1925/1985: 239 History of the Concept of Time).

The four 'Who's' are inter-animating relationships, of the Between, with the potential to become a polyphony, a "plurality of consciousnesses" (Bakhtin, 1929/1963/1984: 6). The polyphony of unmerged voices "in the unity of the event" (IBID.). The problem of polyphony is the four who I introduce next, can become monological (they can take over the dialogical). For genuine polyphony to exist, in the unity of the once-occurrent event (Bakhtin 1919-1921/1985-1986/1993) the polyphony of equally valued consciousnesses remains unmerged, and not given over to one particular ideological view.

True Storytelling® explores this relationship of polyphony freeing itself from monology. An example is stakeholder theory. Stakeholder theory becomes a monologized consciousness, the takeover of polyphony by a "single unified authored consciousness" (Bakhtin, 1929/1963/1984: 9).

Between The Tamara-land of audience connections, relationships, and networks of the entrepreneur's journey.

Our spaces here, there, and yonder in Tamara-land (Boje, 1995), chasing stories from room to room. We are telling and recalling, dwelling together telling and listening together to what storytelling is telling about the fourfold. The fourfold of existence, sky, and earth, divinities and mortals, in which "space is in essence that for which room has been made, that which let into its bonds" we gather-telling and together-listening in the spatial and extension of Tamara-land (Heidegger, 1971 PLT, 152, 154). We 'gather together,' but are we thinking? The yonder locations already pervade the rooms of Tamara-land as we traverse through it, from room to room. The location makes rooms fourfold, in double space-making: (1) the mansion with many rooms in-dwelling, and (2) the building of such room locations that allow space for joining spatial and as an extension. If we can think about where we are right now, that thinking belongs to bridging location to location, room to room, things among things, and what is already pervading the fourfold. Letting-dwell commons the fourfold as "we try to think" (PLT, 156) in that process of together-telling and together-listening that is not just the architecture or the engineering of Tamara-land, but the letting-dwell sets earth and sky (heaven), about divinities and mortals, in "their journey through time" (PLT, 158). Perhaps Pondy's 'enthinking' process, this attempt at thinking becomes a way of questioning that is more than the wording of thought, more than language games.

Practical Training: Using Artifacts and Sand Tray for Entrepreneurial Storytelling

Creating powerful connections with your audience through storytelling requires practice, creativity, and the right tools. One effective training exercise is working with artifacts and a sand tray to visually and tangibly explore the **Four Whos** (Ego-Who, Social-Who, Corporate-Who, and Ecological-Who) and how they relate to your storytelling.

Step 1: Gather Your Artifacts

Start by collecting a variety of small, symbolic items. These can come from anywhere—your children's toy box, desk drawer, or household items. Aim for 20–40 artifacts, each about 3–5 inches in size. Examples include:
- Marbles
- Small stones
- Pieces of Play-Doh
- Pipe cleaners
- Miniature figurines

These artifacts will serve as representations of key aspects of your entrepreneurial story and your audience.

Step 2: Set Up Your Sand Tray
Find a shallow box with plastic sides and fill it with clean, healthy sand. This tray will be your canvas for arranging the artifacts to build a visual representation of your story.

Step 3: Map the Four Who's
Using the artifacts, create four distinct sections in your sand tray to represent the Four Who's:

- **Ego-Who**: Choose artifacts that symbolize your entrepreneurial journey. This is your story—your challenges, successes, and individuality as an entrepreneur.
Example: A marble to symbolize resilience or a small trophy to represent a major achievement.
- **Social-Who**: Add artifacts that represent your relationships, networks, and community connections.
Example: A pipe cleaner shaped like a heart to signify collaboration or a miniature figure representing key mentors.
- **Corporate-Who**: Include items that reflect the institutions or organizations you engage with in your entrepreneurial journey.
Example: A small block to symbolize stability or a coin to represent financial systems.
- **Ecological-Who**: Incorporate artifacts that align with your ecological orientation or sustainability goals.

Example: A green leaf to signify eco-consciousness or a stone to represent grounding in natural resources.

Step 4: Customize for Your Audience
Now, focus on the specific audience you wish to reach with your entrepreneurial story:
- Remove artifacts that aren't relevant to this particular communication.
- Add new artifacts that represent the values, needs, and perspectives of your target audience.
1. Example: A figurine representing your customers or a globe to symbolize a global market.

Imagine this audience and how your storytelling can address their aspirations and challenges.

Step 5: Create Scenes and Storyboards
After arranging the artifacts, visualize how they would appear in the narrative of your entrepreneurial journey. To bring this to life, create a **storyboard**:
- **Sketch or Draw**: Illustrate scenes that reflect the relationship between the Four Whos and your audience.
- **Combine Text and Images**: Use captions or labels to describe the purpose of each artifact and scene.
- **Digital Tools**: Leverage AI tools like ChatGPT or image-generation platforms to create visual elements for your storyboard.

The goal is to connect the dots between your values, your audience's needs, and the message you want to convey.

Step 6: Practice and Refine
Engage in these storytelling practices regularly:
- Identify your audience and revisit the Four Who's.
- Adjust your artifacts and sand tray arrangement as your priorities shift.
- Refine your storyboard with new ideas and visual enhancements.

Each iteration of this exercise deepens your understanding of how to communicate effectively with your audience.

Combining Scenography and Antenarrative Processes
This exercise integrates **True Storytelling® principles** with **Antenarrative Processes**, emphasizing the importance of scenography (the visual and sensory staging of your narrative) and artifacts in crafting immersive storytelling experiences. By using the sand tray and storyboard techniques, you'll develop a practical framework to:
2. Identify and connect with your audience.
3. Leverage the Four Whos and Four Hearts.
4. Build impactful, visually engaging narratives.

Final Thoughts

In entrepreneurial storytelling, the connection between your values, your audience's needs, and the artifacts you use to stage your story is crucial. By training with these techniques, you'll refine your ability to deliver a narrative that resonates deeply, builds trust, and inspires action. Start with the sand tray, develop your storyboard, and let your entrepreneurial journey come to life in vivid, meaningful ways.

Chapter 7: "Reflecting How Stories Create Value by Exploring What's Beyond the Status Quo"

Introduction: The Power of Going Beyond
Entrepreneurship is not just about numbers, metrics, or calculated strategies—it's about stepping into the unknown, embracing intuition, and fostering connections that go beyond the surface. This chapter is your

guide to unlocking the "Beyond" in your entrepreneurial journey through reflection, serendipity, and meaningful storytelling.

Going Beyond means listening to the silence, embracing the vibrations of life, and tuning into a deeper sense of awareness—what we call **enthinkment**. It's about exploring the relationships between what is known and unknown, between rationality and intuition, and using this understanding to create transformative connections in your business.

Movie Script: Go Beyond and Reflect on Your Journey

Scene:

Northern Denmark, on a starlit night under a full moon.
Alvida, David, Hilda, and Sophie stand atop a mountain, gazing at the vast sky. The crisp air is filled with possibility.
Alvida: "Look at the stars. It's like they're calling us to step into the unknown, to go beyond what we can see and touch."
David: "Yes, and that's the essence of the Beyond. It's not just about goals or plans—it's about embracing the mystery, reflecting deeply, and being open to what comes next."
Hilda: "The Beyond is a sacred space, a place where stories are written in silence and the unseen guides our steps. It's where true transformation begins."
Sophie: "I feel it—like I'm standing on the edge of a new adventure. But where do I leap from here? How do I make the unknown a reality?"
Alvida: "The answer lies in reflection. Let's begin by revisiting the stories that brought us here and imagining the ones we'll create next."

The Plot Twist

[Suddenly, the sound of a melodic hum rises from the valley below. A glowing light appears, illuminating an ancient stone circle nearby. The group exchanges curious glances.]

Hilda: "This... this is unexpected. That stone circle hasn't glowed in centuries."
David: "It's as if it's responding to us. Perhaps it's inviting us to reflect and reimagine the stories we tell."
Sophie: "Let's go. This might be the key to unlocking the Beyond."
[The group moves toward the glowing circle, standing at its center. As they close their eyes, the hum deepens, and they are transported to a dreamlike realm where they see visions of their past, present, and future intertwined.]

Surprise Ending: The Revelation
[The visions fade, leaving each of them with a small glowing artifact in their hands. Hilda steps forward, holding a luminous orb.]
Hilda: "This is the gift of the Beyond. It's not a map or a plan—it's a mirror of your potential. To harness it, you must choose your next adventure."
Alvida: "But which path do we choose? How do we know what's next?"
Hilda: "The choice is yours, but each path requires courage and commitment. Here are your options:"

1. **Embrace the Unknown:** Follow the path of serendipity. Let intuition guide you to new opportunities and let your curiosity lead you to unexpected discoveries. **Exercise:** Begin each day by writing down three intuitive thoughts or hunches and act on one of them.
2. **Build New Connections:** Expand your network and learn from others. Collaborate with people whose experiences differ from yours. **Exercise:** Create a "connection map" of five individuals or organizations you want to learn from and reach out to them.
3. **Shape the Future Through Storytelling:** Use antenarrative storytelling to visualize and narrate the future you want to create. **Exercise:** Write a story set five years in the future where your goals have been achieved. Identify the steps needed to make it a reality.

Resolution: The Leap Forward

[The group steps out of the stone circle, each clutching their artifact. The glowing light fades, leaving only the stars above.]

Sophie: "I know my choice. I'll embrace the unknown. It's time to trust my instincts and see where they lead me."

Alvida: "I'll build new connections. Sharing stories and learning from others will make my vision stronger."

David: "For me, it's shaping the future. Through storytelling, I'll create the reality I want to see."

Hilda: "And so the journey continues. Remember, the Beyond isn't a destination—it's a state of being. Reflect, connect, and leap boldly."

[The group begins their descent, the night sky their guide. Each step forward feels lighter, filled with possibility.]

Closing Narration

Voiceover (David): "As entrepreneurs, we're not just builders of businesses—we're creators of stories, navigators of the unknown, and architects of the future. The Beyond calls us to reflect, to connect, and to take bold steps into what could be.

Which path will you choose? The unknown, new connections, or shaping the future? The choice is yours, and the journey is just beginning."

[The camera pans up to the stars, fading to black as the hum from the stone circle lingers in the air.]

The End.

Reflecting on Stories: Create Value by unconcealing the Beyond

Stories are more than just narratives—they are bridges between what we know and what we can imagine. Reflect on the stories that have shaped your entrepreneurial path:

1. **Look Back:** What past experiences brought unexpected opportunities? Recall moments when intuition led to success.
2. **Be Present:** Identify the vibes or feelings you experience when engaging with your customers or team. What "vibrations" signal you're on the right path?

3. **Look Ahead:** Envision the futures you're shaping. What story are you writing for your customers, and how does it unfold beyond the present?

Practical Tip: Create a reflection journal where you document moments of serendipity or unexpected inspiration. Use these entries to uncover patterns that guide your next steps.

Harnessing Enthinkment: The Practice of Thinking Beyond

Enthinkment is about engaging a different depth of thinking, one that goes beyond rational calculations and taps into intuition and the unseen. Entrepreneurs often rely on "gut feelings" or hunches—this is enthinkment in action.

How to Practice Enthinkment:

- **Pause and Reflect:** Before making major decisions, take a moment to reflect deeply. Listen to the "other hand clapping," as Lou Pondy suggests. What insights emerge in the silence?
- **Dance Between Ideas:** Like dancing partners, explore your challenges from different perspectives. What does your problem look like through your customer's eyes? Through your competitors? Through a mentor's?
- **Follow the Signs:** Pay attention to unexpected opportunities—serendipitous moments that might seem minor but hold potential.

Exercise: Try the "Dancing Partners" technique. Write down your current challenge and approach it through the lens of another business or framework. Shift perspectives and reflect on the insights gained.

Serendipity as a Strategic Tool

Serendipity is often undervalued in entrepreneurship. It's the art of recognizing opportunities when they appear unexpectedly. Success often stems from following a path that wasn't planned but felt right.

How to Cultivate Serendipity:

- **Stay Curious:** Keep an open mind to new ideas and unexpected possibilities.
- **Trust Your Intuition:** When something feels right, explore it further.

- **Connect the Dots:** Reflect on how seemingly unrelated events or ideas might work together.

Practical Tip: Form a storytelling circle with peers. Share moments of serendipity and how they influenced your journey. This practice builds collective wisdom and inspiration.

The Four Hearts and Going Beyond

The four hearts—**Beneath, Before, Bets, and Beyond**—are essential to true storytelling and reflection:
- **Beneath:** Connect with your values and passions. Ask yourself: How do my values shape my entrepreneurial decisions?
- **Before:** Reflect on the moments and experiences that shaped your journey. What lessons can you carry forward?
- **Bets:** Consider your bets on the future. What risks are you taking, and how are they aligned with your vision?
- **Beyond:** Step into the unknown. Explore possibilities that are not immediately evident but hold potential.

Practical Tip: Use a vision board or artifact collection to represent each heart. Physically arranging these items can help you visualize your journey and align your next steps.

Storytelling Circles: A Tool for Reflection and Growth

Gather a small group of trusted peers or mentors and create a storytelling circle. The purpose is to share and reflect on personal and professional experiences, focusing on the serendipity, intuition, and lessons learned.

How to Run a Storytelling Circle:
- **Set the Stage:** Choose a comfortable, distraction-free environment.
- **Share Stories:** Each participant shares a story about an unexpected success or challenge.
- **Reflect Together:** Discuss common themes, lessons, and insights.
- **Document Learnings:** Write down key takeaways and actionable steps.

Example: Sophie, a young entrepreneur, discovered through a storytelling circle that her best ideas often emerged during nature walks. She began incorporating daily walks into her routine, leading to more innovative solutions.

Exercises for Entrepreneurs to Go Beyond

- **The Sand Tray Exercise:**

Collect small artifacts that represent your ego, social connections, corporate influences, and ecological concerns.

Arrange them in a sand tray or on a surface, reflecting on how they interact.

Remove items that no longer serve your entrepreneurial vision and add new ones that align with your goals.

- **Storyboard Your Journey:**

Create a visual map of your entrepreneurial story. Include past milestones, current challenges, and future aspirations.

Use sketches, photos, or digital tools to bring your storyboard to life.

- **Follow the Signs:**

Document moments when you felt a strong intuitive pull. What patterns do you notice? How can you intentionally create space for these moments?

Embracing the Abyss: Finding Strength in the Unknown

The unknown can feel like an abyss, but it is also a space of infinite potential. Reflect on your journey with courage and curiosity. Embrace the silence, listen to the vibrations around you, and follow the serendipitous paths that emerge.

Practical Tip: Dedicate time each week to deep reflection. Disconnect from distractions and focus on the questions: Where am I now? What's next? What am I missing?

Conclusion: Your Entrepreneurial Odyssey

Your entrepreneurial journey is more than a series of calculated steps. It's an unfolding story shaped by intuition, reflection, and connections. By embracing enthinkment, serendipity, and the four hearts, you can navigate the Beyond with confidence and purpose.

As you move forward, remember the wisdom of this book: **Build meaningful relationships, reflect deeply, and stay open to the possibilities that lie just beyond the horizon.** Your story is still unfolding—make it extraordinary.

References

Antenarrative Publications (see over 70 at https://antenarrativ.com)

Boje, D. M. (2001). Narrative Methods for Organizational and Communication Research. London: Sage.
Boje, D. M. (2007). The antenarrative turn in narrative studies. Communicative Practices in Workplaces and the Professions: Cultural Perspectives on the Regulation of Discourse and Organizations, 219-237.
Boje, D. M. (2011a). Introduction to agential antenarratives that shape the future of organizations. In Storytelling and the Future of Organizations (pp. 1-19). Routledge.
Boje, D. M. (2011b). The antenarrative process: A theory of storytelling and organizational change. Journal of Management Inquiry, 20(2), 143-155. doi: 10.1177/1056492610383114
Boje, D. M. (2012). Reflections: What does the quantum physics of storytelling mean for change management? Journal of Change Management, 12(3), 253-271.
Boje, D. M. (2013). The seven antenarrative processes: A framework for understanding organizational storytelling. Journal of Organizational Change Management, 26(3), 433-446. doi: 10.1108/JOCM-02-2013-0014
Boje, D. M. (2015). Antenarrative and the art of storytelling in organizations. Journal of Business Research, 68(1), 1-8. doi: 10.1016/j.jbusres.2014.10.011
Boje, D. M. (2024). True Storytelling Antenarrative-Processes and the Existential-Ethics Turn. In A World Scientific Encyclopedia of Business Storytelling Set 2: Methodologies and Big Data Analysis of Business Storytelling Volume 1: Business True Storytelling (pp. 43-58).
Boje, D., Cast, M., & Saylors, R. (2014). Liquid times for the entrepreneurial identity non-profit organization. In Liquid Organization (pp. 140-152). Routledge.
Boje, D. M., Haley, U. C., & Saylors, R. (2016). Antenarratives of organizational change: The microstoria of Burger King's storytelling in space, time and strategic context. Human Relations, 69(2), 391-418.
Boje, D. M., Helmuth, C. A., & Saylors, R. (2013). Cameo: Spinning authentic leadership living stories of the self. In Authentic Leadership (pp. 271-278). Edward Elgar Publishing.

Boje, D. M., & Henderson, T. L. (Eds.). (2014). Being Quantum: Ontological Storytelling in the Age of Antenarrative. Cambridge Scholars Publishing.

Boje, D. M., & Rosile, G. A. (2020). How to Use Conversational Storytelling Interviews for Your Dissertation. Edward Elgar Publishing.

Boje, D. M., & Rosile, G. A. (2022). The storytelling science paradigm: Evoking the transformative power of Indigenous ontological antenarratives in curious conversation. In Transcendent Development: The Ethics of Universal Dignity (pp. 15-42). Emerald Publishing Limited.

Boje, D. M., & Saylors, R. (2015). The future of history. The Routledge Companion to Management and Organizational History, 197-206.

Boje, D. M., & Saylors, R. (2024). The Management Thought of Louis R. Pondy: Reclaiming the Enthinkment Path. Taylor & Francis.

Boje, D. M., Svane, M., & Gergerich, E. M. (2016). Counternarrative and antenarrative inquiry in two cross-cultural contexts. European Journal of Cross-Cultural Competence and Management, 4(1), 55-84.

Danish Entrepreneurs

Bjerregaard, T. (2018). The entrepreneurial journey: A narrative approach. Journal of Entrepreneurship and Public Policy, 7(2), 141-155. doi: 10.1108/JEPP-02-2018-0014

Mikkelsen, K. (2017). The role of storytelling in entrepreneurial identity formation. Journal of Small Business and Entrepreneurship, 30(2), 147-162. doi: 10.1080/08276331.2017.1281445

US Entrepreneurs

Hoffman, R. (2012). The startup of you: Adapt to the future, invest in yourself, and transform your career. Crown Business.

Schultz, H. (2011). Pour your heart into it: How Starbucks built a company one cup at a time. Hyperion.

Svane, M. (2015). The startup way: How entrepreneurs can become successful leaders by leveraging the startup strategy. Wiley.

Hoffman, J. (2018). The entrepreneurial journey: A narrative approach. Journal of Entrepreneurship and Public Policy, 7(2), 141-155. doi: 10.1108/JEPP-02-2018-0014

Koch, A. (2017). The role of storytelling in entrepreneurial identity formation. Journal of Small Business and Entrepreneurship, 30(2), 147-162. doi: 10.1080/08276331.2017.1281445

Note: The references provided are a selection of publications on antenarrative and entrepreneurial storytelling and are not an exhaustive list. See https://antenarrative.com for over 70 publications. Additionally, the references to Danish and American entrepreneurs are a selection of well-known entrepreneurs and are not an exhaustive list.

The Concluding Reflections and Insights

(The scene is set in a cozy café in Copenhagen, where David Boje, Alvida the actress, Hilda the shaman, and Sophie from Denmark, who has been coached by the trio, sit around a table, sipping their coffee and reflecting on their journey.)

David Boje: "Sophie, you've come a long way in crafting your entrepreneurial story. What do you think are the most important insights you've gained from our coaching sessions?"

Sophie: "I think it's the understanding of the seven antenarrative processes. It's helped me to see my story in a new light. I used to think my story was just about me and my business, but now I see it as a complex web of connections between humans and non-humans, and the spaces in between."

Alvida: "Ah, yes! The spaces in between are where the magic happens. It's where we find the hidden patterns and meanings that shape our stories."

Hilda: "And it's not just about the stories we tell, but also the stories we don't tell. The beneath, the before, the bets on the future – all these antenarrative processes are crucial in shaping our entrepreneurial journeys."

David Boje: "Exactly! The seven antenarrative processes offer a framework for entrepreneurs to explore and make sense of their experiences. By examining the beneath, the before, and the bets on the future, entrepreneurs can uncover the underlying narratives that drive their decisions and actions."

Sophie: "I see what you mean. For me, it's been about recognizing the patterns and themes that have emerged in my business. By acknowledging the beneath, the before, and the bets on the future, I've been able to make more informed decisions and create a more compelling story for my customers."

Alvida: "And it's not just about the entrepreneurs themselves, but also about the impact they have on others. The becoming of transformation, the between humans and non-humans – these are all critical aspects of entrepreneurial storytelling."

Hilda: "I think that's what makes this guide so powerful. It's not just a tool for entrepreneurs, but also for anyone who wants to understand the complexities of human experience. By exploring the seven antenarrative processes, we can gain a deeper understanding of ourselves and our place in the world."

David Boje: "That's right. The Danish and American Guide to Crafting Compelling Entrepreneur-Storytelling using the Seven Antenarrative Processes is a valuable resource for anyone looking to create a more authentic and compelling story. By embracing the complexities of the human experience, entrepreneurs can create a more meaningful and impactful story that resonates with their audience."

Sophie: "I couldn't agree more. This guide has been a game-changer for me. I feel more confident in my ability to tell my story and connect with my customers on a deeper level."

Alvida: "And that's what it's all about – connection. When we share our stories, we connect with others on a deeper level. We build trust, we build relationships, and we build a sense of community."

Hilda: "So, let's raise a cup to the power of storytelling and the seven antenarrative processes. May they continue to inspire and guide entrepreneurs and storytellers alike."
(The group raises their cups in a toast, as the conversation continues, exploring the many ways in which storytelling can shape our lives and our businesses.)

Practical Tips for Using the Seven Antenarrative Processes in Entrepreneurial Storytelling
1. **The Beneath**: Explore the underlying motivations and values that drive your business. What are your core values? What drives your passion for your work?
2. **The Before**: Reflect on the experiences and events that have shaped your business. What challenges have you faced? How have you overcome them?
3. **The Bets on the Future**: Think about the risks and uncertainties that lie ahead. What are your hopes and dreams for your business? What are you willing to bet on?

4. **The Being in Space-Time-Mattering**: Consider the spaces and times in which your business operates. How do you create value in those spaces? How do you make a difference in people's lives?
5. **The Becoming of Transformation**: Think about the transformations that have occurred in your business. How have you grown and evolved as an entrepreneur? What lessons have you learned along the way?
6. **The Between Humans and Non-Humans**: Explore the relationships between humans and non-humans in your business. How do you work with partners, suppliers, and customers? How do you create value through those relationships?
7. **The Beyond**: Consider the unknowns and uncertainties that lie ahead. What are the biggest risks and challenges facing your business? How will you adapt and evolve to meet those challenges?

By incorporating these seven antenarrative processes into your entrepreneurial storytelling, you can create a more compelling and authentic story that resonates with your audience. Remember to be honest, vulnerable, and authentic in your storytelling, and to use the processes as a framework for exploring the complexities of your business and your entrepreneurial journey.

Co-authored with Rohny Saylors

The following image is from the Boje & Saylors book:

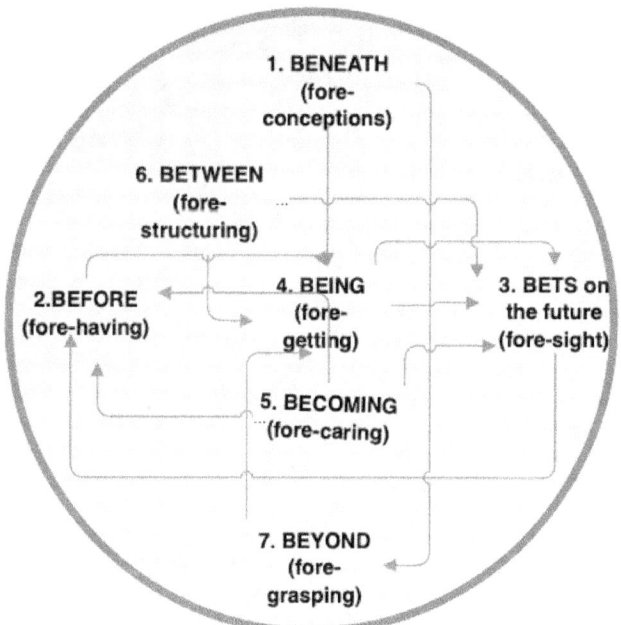

7 Antenarrative Processes of the Fore-Times-in-Advance

The 70+ Antenarrative Publications

Explore the latest research and thinking in antenarrative theory and methodology. Our work spans organizational studies, storytelling, and narrative analysis. The Boje, D. M. & Saylors, R. (2024). *The Management Thought of Louis R. Pondy: Reclaiming the Enthinkment Path*. Taylor & Francis is the most up-to-date treatment of antenarratives,

the seeds of storytelling. There is a myriad of antenarrative storytelling process studies (over 70), but surprisingly very few are situated to contribute to the studies of haute cuisine innovation. For example, just four antenarrative storytelling process studies have been applied to haute cuisine (Stierand et al., 2019; Bounty, Gomez, & Stierand, 2018; Feuls et al.,2019). Only studies (Boje, Haley & Saylors, 2016) applied antenarrative storytelling to fast food, and only four studies applied antenarrative processes to entrepreneurship (Verduyn & Jansen, 2005; Saylors, 2012; Saylors, Boje, & Mueller, 2014; Phillips, Moore & Rutherford, 20205, in press).

Here is the list of 70 plus Antenarrative publications

1. Agar, Michael. (2005). Telling it like you think it might be. E: CO Issue Vol. 7 Nos. 3-4 2005 pp. 23-34. https://www.researchgate.net/profile/Michael-Agar-3/publication/255012946_Telling_it_like_you_think_it_might_be_Narrative_linguistic_anthropology_and_the_complex_organization/links/

53f7c30b0cf2823e5bdbd5b7/Telling-it-like-you-think-it-might-be-Narrative-linguistic-anthropology-and-the-complex-organization.pdf

2. Alexander, J. J., & Edenfield, A. C. (2024). Erased by Design: An Antenarrative of Ellenton and the Savannah River Plant. *Technical Communication, 71*(1), 7-19.

3. Anderson, R. B. (2019). Challenging a Culture of Secrecy: 217Investigating the Emergence of Antenarrative Storytelling in Community Responses to the Hanford Nuclear Reservation. In *Networking Argument* (pp. 217-223). Routledge.

4. Auvinen, T., Sajasalo, P., Sintonen, T., Takala, T., & Järvenpää, M. (2018). Antenarratives in Ongoing Strategic Change: Using the Story Index to Capture Daunting and Optimistic Futures. In H. Krämer, & M. Wenzel (Eds.), How Organizations Manage the Future: Theoretical Perspectives and Empirical Insights (pp. 133-151). Palgrave Macmillan. https://doi.org/10.1007/978-3-319-74506-0_7

5. Barge, J. Kevin. "Antenarrative and managerial practice." *Communication Studies* 55.1 (2004): 106-127.

6. Betts, T., Hintz, E. A., & Buzzanell, P. M. (2022). Emplotting anticipatory resilience: An antenarrative extension of the communication theory of resilience. *Communication Monographs, 89*(2), 211-234.

7. Blum, V., & Gumb, B. (2016). Antenarrative and financial communication: lessons from the Areva/UraMin operation. *Comptabilite-Controle-Audit, 22*(2), 77-107.

8. Boje, D.M. (2001). Narrative Methods for Organizational and Communication Research. London: Sage.

9. Boje, D. M. (2007). The antenarrative turn in narrative studies. *Communicative practices in workplaces and the professions: Cultural perspectives on the regulation of discourse and organizations*, 219-237.

10. Boje, D. M. (2011). Introduction to agential antenarratives that shape the future of organizations. In *Storytelling and the Future of Organizations* (pp. 1-19). Routledge.

11. Boje, D. M. (2012). Reflections: What does the quantum physics of storytelling mean for change management? *Journal of Change Management, 12*(3), 253-271.

12. Boje, D. M. (2024). True Storytelling Antenarrative-Processes and the Existential-Ethics Turn. In *A World Scientific Encyclopedia of Business Storytelling Set 2: Methodologies and Big Data Analysis of Business Storytelling Volume 1: Business True Storytelling* (pp. 43-58).

13. Boje, D., Cast, M., & Saylors, R. (2014). Liquid times for the entrepreneurial identity non-profit organization. In *Liquid Organization* (pp. 140-152). Routledge.

14. Boje, D. M., Haley, U. C., & Saylors, R. (2016). Antenarratives of organizational change: The microstoria of Burger King's storytelling in space, time and strategic context. *human relations*, *69*(2), 391-418.

15. Boje, D. M., Helmuth, C. A., & Saylors, R. (2013). Cameo: Spinning authentic leadership living stories of the self. In *Authentic Leadership* (pp. 271-278). Edward Elgar Publishing.

16. Boje, D. M., & Henderson, T. L. (Eds.). (2014). *Being quantum: Ontological storytelling in the age of antenarrative*. Cambridge Scholars Publishing.

17. Boje, D., & Rosile, G. A. (2020). *How to use conversational storytelling interviews for your dissertation*. Edward Elgar Publishing.

18. Boje, D. M., & Rosile, G. A. (2022). The storytelling science paradigm: Evoking the transformative power of Indigenous ontological antenarratives in curious conversation. In *Transcendent development: The ethics of universal dignity* (pp. 15-42). Emerald Publishing Limited.

19. Boje, D. M., & Saylors, R. (2015). The future of history. *The Routledge Companion to Management and Organizational History*, 197-206.

20. Boje, D. M. & Saylors, R. (2024). *The Management Thought of Louis R. Pondy: Reclaiming the Enthinkment Path*. Taylor & Francis.

21. Boje, D. M., Svane, M., & Gergerich, E. M. (2016). Counternarrative and antenarrative inquiry in two cross-cultural contexts. *European Journal of Cross-Cultural Competence and Management, 4*(1), 55-84.

22. Bouty, I., Gomez, M. L., & Stierand, M. (2018). The creative leadership practices of haute cuisine chefs. In *Creative Leadership* (pp. 156-170). Routledge.

23. Connor, T., & Phelan, L. (2015). Antenarrative and transnational labor rights activism: Making sense of complexity and ambiguity in the interaction between global social movements and global corporations. *Globalizations, 12*(2), 149-163.

24. Dalcher, D., & Drevin, L. (2004). Learning from information systems failures by using narrative and ante-narrative methods. *South African Computer Journal*, (33), 88-97.

25. Dorpenyo, I. K. (2022). Local knowledge as illiterate rhetoric: An antenarrative approach to enacting socially just technical communication. *Journal of Technical Writing and Communication, 52*(3), 291-315.

26. Feuls, M., Stierand, M. B., Dörfler, V., Boje, D. M., & Haley, U. C. (2019, September). Exploring practices of managing creativity: a qualitative meta-analysis of narratives from haute cuisine. In *CINet 2019: 20th International Conference on Innovating in an Era of Continuous Disruption*.

27. Flora, J., Boje, D., & Ann, G. Rosile, Kenneth Hacker. (2016). Journal of Veterans Studies. Vol 1, No 1 Theoretical and Applied Review of Embodied Restorying for Post-Deployment Family.

28. Frandsen, S., Svane, M., & Maria Humle, D. (2023). Who is responsible—And for what? An antenarrative perspective on organizational members' crisis sensemaking of responsibility during a corporate scandal. *Human relations*, pp. 1-23 00187267231205781.

29. Fu, X. (2018). The ante-narrative on bronze wares and the Chinese narrative tradition. *Neohelicon, 45*, 191-212.

30. Horvath, I., Beeler, B., & Bonnet, M. (2022). A storytelling interpretation of the socio-economic theory: Example of an

intervention-research in a theater company. *Revue de gestion des ressources humaines*, (4), 3-19.

31. Jones, Natasha N., Kristen R. Moore, and Rebecca Walton (2016). Disrupting the past to disrupt the future: An antenarrative of technical communication. *Technical Communication Quarterly* 25, no. 4: 211-229.

32. Jørgensen, K. M. (2009). Genealogies of Becoming: Antenarrative Inquiry in Organizations. *Tamara: journal of critical postmodern organization science*, 8(1), 32-47.

33. Jørgensen, K. M., & Boje, D. M. (2020). Storytelling sustainability in problem-based learning. *Populism and higher education curriculum development: Problem based learning as a mitigating response*, 369-391.

34. Larsen, Jens. (2024). True Storytelling—A Philosophy of Life and an Ethical Change-management Method. In *A World Scientific Encyclopedia of Business Storytelling Set 2: Methodologies and Big Data Analysis of Business Storytelling Volume 1: Business True Storytelling* (pp. 1-16).

35. Larsen, Jens; Boje, D. M.; Bruun, Lena. (2021). True Storytelling: Seven Principles for an Ethical and Sustainable Change-Management Strategy. London: Routledge.

36. LeFebvre, L., & Blackburn, K. (2012). Choosing Emma's ending: Exploring the intersection of small and big stories, antenarrative, and narrative. *Narrative Inquiry, 22*(2), 211-225

37. Lueg, K., & Rennstam, J. (2023). How knowledge moves across social fields: A conceptual illustration of the antenarrative field of economic degrowth thinking. In *Perspectives on Knowledge Communication* (pp. 215-231). Routledge.

38. Lundholt, M. W., & Boje, D. (2018). Understanding organizational narrative-counter-narratives dynamics: An overview of Communication Constitutes Organization (CCO) and Storytelling Organization Theory (SOT) approaches. *Communication and Language at Work, 5*(1), 18-29

39. Massoud, J. A., Boje, D. M., Capener, E., & Marcillo, M. (2019). Intertextual analysis of the BP Prudhoe Bay disaster: applying the 5 Bs of antenarrative. *International Journal of Organizational Analysis, 27*(5), 1562-1577.

40. Petersen, E. J., & Moeller, R. M. (2016). Using antenarrative to uncover systems of power in mid-20th century policies on marriage and maternity at IBM. *Journal of Technical Writing and Communication, 46*(3), 362-386.

41. Petersen, E. J. (2020). Women's lived experience as authority: Antenarratives and interactional power as tools for

engagement. *Dialogue: A Journal of Mormon Thought, 53*(1), 47-74.

42. Phillips, D., Moore, C. B., & Rutherford, M. W. (2025, in press). Legitimating language and emotional tone in antenarratives: A cultural entrepreneurship perspective. *Journal of Business Research, 186*, 114988. https://www.sciencedirect.com/science/article/pii/S0148296324004922?casa_token=Wz_Wpra3fz0AAAAA:S3OMQ1Zxi0Q-bAiZLaX8td9zbhyVWrrdwwqBNiiFQOUx5gX57FmzsAzmPepye66rRjHTK4YCW7qt

43. Poudel, D. (2019). Making Sense or Betting on the Future? Identifying Antenarratives of AI Projects in a Large Financial Organization. *Electronic Journal of Business Ethics and Organization Studies, 24*(2): 20-33.http://ejbo.jyu.fi/pdf/ejbo_vol24_no2_pages_20-33.pdf

44. Rosile, G. A., & Boardman, C. (2011). Antenarrative ethics of native American Indian trading. *2011 Proceedings 20 Years of Storytelling and sc'MOI: A Celebration*, 180-.

45. Rosile, G. A., Boje, D. M., Carlon, D. M., Downs, A., & Saylors, R. (2013). Storytelling diamond: An antenarrative integration of the six facets of storytelling in organization research design. *Organizational Research Methods, 16*(4), 557-580.

46. Rosile, G. A., M Boje, D., & Claw, C. M. (2018). Ensemble leadership theory: Collectivist, relational, and heterarchical roots from indigenous contexts. *Leadership, 14*(3), 307-328.

47. Sandham, S., & Fuller, G. (2020). The 'Damore Memo': what is the value of antenarrative in organizational communication? *Continuum, 34*(3), 431-447.

48. Saylors, Jillian. (2018). Revealing Antenarratives in the Autism of Quantum Storytelling. In *The Emerald Handbook of Quantum Storytelling Consulting* (pp. 99-111). Emerald Publishing Limited.

49. Saylors, R. (2012, July). The Antenarrative of Illicit Market Entrepreneurs an Autoethnography of Metanoia Experiences. In *Academy of Management Proceedings* (Vol. 2012, No. 1, p. 16934). Briarcliff Manor, NY 10510: Academy of Management.

50. Saylors, R., Boje, D. M., & Mueller, T. J. (2014). Entrepreneurial Storytelling in Moments of Friendship: Antenarratives of business plans, risk-taking, and venture capital narratives. *Tamara Journal for Critical Organization Inquiry, 12*(4): 3-15. https://journals.kozminski.edu.pl/pl/system/files/395-1387-1-PB.pdf

51. Seloti, S. L., & Alves, M. A. (2011). Antenarratives, Strategic Alliances, and Sensemaking: Engagement and Divorce Without

Marriage Between Two Brazilian Air Carrier Firms. In *Storytelling and the future of organizations* (pp. 176-187). Routledge.

52. Shufutinsky, A., & Burrell, D. N. (2024). Storytelling When the Source of the Story Is Unavailable: The Multi-Bystander Interpretive Storytelling Approach. In *A World Scientific Encyclopedia of Business Storytelling Set 2: Methodologies and Big Data Analysis of Business Storytelling Volume 5: Business Storytelling and Grounding Methodology* (pp. 79-115)

53. Shufutinsky, A., Svane, M. S., & Boje, D. M. (2024). Introduction to Grounding Methodology in Business Storytelling. In *A World Scientific Encyclopedia of Business Storytelling Set 2: Methodologies and Big Data Analysis of Business Storytelling Volume 5: Business Storytelling and Grounding Methodology* (pp. 1-11). https://www.worldscientific.com/doi/pdf/10.1142/9789811280962_0001

54. Sliwa, M., & Cairns, G. (2007). Exploring narratives and antenarratives of graffiti artists: beyond dichotomies of commitment and detachment. *Culture and Organization, 13*(1), 73-82.

55. Sparre, M., & Boje, D. M. (2020). Utilizing participative action research with storytelling interventions to create sustainability in Danish farming. *Leadership & Organization Development*

Journal, *38*(4), 41-54. https://davidboje.com/vita/paper_pdfs/Sparre%20and%20Boje-edited.pdf

56. Stierand, M., Boje, D. M., Glăveanu, V., Dörfler, V., Haley, U. C., & Feuls, M. (2019). Paradoxes of "creativity": Examining the creative process through an antenarrative lens. *The Journal of Creative Behavior*, *53*(2), 165-170.

57. Svane, M., Gergerich, E., & Boje, D. M. (2016). Fractal change management and counter-narrative in cross-cultural change. In *Counter-narratives and organization* (pp. 129-154). Routledge.

58. Strand, Anete M. C. (2012). Enacting the Between. *On dis/continuous intra-active becoming of/through an Apparatus of Material Storytelling. Book 2 How to Build an Oasis with a Good Organizational Becoming through an Apparatus of Material Storytelling*. https://vbn.aau.dk/files/229677225/Entangling_Organizations_paper_Anete_Strand_1312_2015.pdf

59. Svane, M. (2019). Antenarratives and Heteroglossia in Organizational Storytelling: A Living Medium Shaping the Future of Organizations in the Quantum Age. *Communication & Language at Work*, *6*(1), 63-77.

60. Tyler, J. A. (2011). Living story and antenarrative in organizational accidents. In *Storytelling and the Future of Organizations* (pp. 137-147). Routledge.

61. Tyler, J. A., & Swartz, A. L. (2012). Storytelling and transformative learning. *The Handbook of transformative learning: Theory, research, and practice*, 455-470

62. Vaara, E., Sonenshein, S., & Boje, D. (2016). Narratives as sources of stability and change in organizations: Approaches and directions for future research. *Academy of Management Annals*, *10*(1), 495-560. http://ereserve.library.utah.edu/Annual/MGT/7810/Diekmann/narratives.pdf

63. Vaara, E., & Tienari, J. (2011). On the narrative construction of multinational corporations: An antenarrative analysis of legitimation and resistance in a cross-border merger. *Organization Science*, *22*(S), 370-390.

64. Van Hilten, A., & Ruel, S. (2024). The Chihuahua and the Space Ping in the margins: Antenarratives of two (older) Women Early Career Academics. *Gender, Work & Organization*, *31*(5), 2066-2094.

65. Verduyn, K., & Jansen, P. (2005). Entrepreneurial myths. Using biographies and (Ante) narrative research methods in entrepreneurship education. *International Journal of Entrepreneurship Education*, *3*(3), 229-244.

66. Vickers, M. H. (2005). Illness, work, and organization: Postmodern perspectives, antenarratives, and chaos narratives for the reinstatement of voice. *Tamara Journal of Critical Organisation Inquiry*, *3*(2), 74.

67. Wakefield, T. H. (2012). Beyond social constructionism: ontological antenarratives. Pp. 173-182 in Bente Nørgaard (ed.) *Beyond Sensemaking and Social Constructivist-Narrative*. Accessed Jun 23, 2021,

    at https://core.ac.uk/download/pdf/60531149.pdf#page=178

68. Wan, R. (2014). An Investigation on the Antenarrative in Ancient Chinese Novels. *Theoretical Studies in Literature and Art*, *34*(2), 66-75.

69. Weick, K. E. (2012). Organized sensemaking: A commentary on processes of interpretive work. *Human Relations*, *65*(1), 141-153. Accessed Jun,23 20,21

    at htt,ps://,citeseerx.ist.psu.edu/viewdoc/download?doi=10.1.1.995.5541&rep=rep1&type=pdf

70. Wolgemuth, J. R. (2014). Analyzing for critical resistance in narrative research. *Qualitative Research*, *14*(5), 586-602.

71. Yolles, M. (2007). The dynamics of narrative and antenarrative and their relation to the story.

More resources at ANTENARRATIVE.com and CSIstory.com

www.ingramcontent.com/pod-product-compliance
Lightning Source LLC
Chambersburg PA
CBHW071030240526
45469CB00006BD/2164